D0449748

House Beautiful
COLORS FOR YOUR HOME
300 DESIGNER FAVORITES

House Beautiful
COLORS FOR YOUR HOME
300 DESIGNER FAVORITES

HEARST BOOKS
A division of Sterling Publishing Co., Inc.

New York / London
www.sterlingpublishing.com

Book design by Nancy Leonard

Library of Congress Cataloging-in-Publication Data
House beautiful colors for your home : 300 designer favorites / the editors of House Beautiful. – 1st paperback ed.
    p. cm.
  Includes index.
  ISBN 978-1-58816-739-2
  1. Color in interior decoration. I. House beautiful. II. Title: Colors for your home.
  NK2115.5.C6G34 2008
  747'.94–dc22

                            2008001533

10 9 8 7 6 5 4 3

Published by Hearst Books
A division of Sterling Publishing Co., Inc.
387 Park Avenue South, New York, NY 10016

House Beautiful and Hearst Books are trademarks
of Hearst Communications, Inc.

www.housebeautiful.com

For information about custom editions, special sales,
premium and corporate purchases, please contact
Sterling Special Sales Department at 800-805-5489
or specialsales@sterlingpublishing.com.

Distributed in Canada by Sterling Publishing
c/o Canadian Manda Group, 165 Dufferin Street
Toronto, Ontario, Canada M6K 3H6

Distributed in Australia by Capricorn Link (Australia) Pty. Ltd.
P.O. Box 704, Windsor, NSW 2756 Australia

Manufactured in China

Sterling ISBN 978-1-58816-739-2

MORNING GLORY

UTAH SKY

DARK ROYAL BLUE

WINDMILL WINGS

PALE MOON

COOKING APPLE GREEN

SPRING IRIS

AUTUMN CROCUS

COLONIAL ROSE

 CONTENTS

INTRODUCTION

COLORS FOR YOUR HOME 10

CHAPTER 1

THE BASICS 12

CHAPTER 2

COLORS TO BRIGHTEN YOUR DAY 116

CHAPTER 3

INSPIRATION FROM AROUND THE WORLD 174

COLOR INDEX

ROOM BY ROOM 208

COLOR INDEX

SHADE BY SHADE 231

DESIGNER INDEX 272

INDEX 280

FOWLER PINK

ORIENTAL IRIS

SUNDANCE

SASSY BLUE

PATRIOT BLUE

COLONY GREEN

RIVIERA AZURE

PERIDOT

CORAL GABLES

What's your favorite color?

INTRODUCTION

What's your favorite color?

You've been asked that question hundreds of times, and answered without skipping a beat. It is a very simple question—until it's time to choose a paint color for the walls of your home. Then, all of a sudden, it's surprisingly hard. Who hasn't struggled to pick a cream that wasn't too yellow or a blue that wasn't too cold?

No more struggling. The colors you're looking for are in this book. Based on *House Beautiful*'s most popular column, this little volume is filled with more than 300 paint formulas that professional interior designers have used successfully in their own rooms. It explains why they work and where they work best. These are the colors you've been trying to find— colors you can live with happily for years.

House Beautiful offers its deepest appreciation to all the designers who have shared their hard-earned expertise in color and décor. Their paint selections and commentary provide rare insight into what makes color work. Thanks to their extraordinary generosity, you, too, can make their favorite colors your own.

CHAPTER

1

THE BASICS

TAKING
THE PLUNGE

Timidity can keep you trapped in bland surroundings. Let these fearless designers ease you down a more colorful path. Follow their lead and you'll never turn back.

In a Connecticut lake cottage, designer Gil Schafer and color consultant Eve Ashcraft chose Narragansett Green for the porch's trim and floor, and Stonington Gray for the ceiling, creating a natural transition between indoors and out.

GIL SCHAFER AND EVE ASHCRAFT
BENJAMIN MOORE | NARRAGANSETT GREEN HC-157
| STONINGTON GRAY HC-170

PETER DUNHAM

RALPH LAUREN PAINT | OYSTER BAY SS61

"Take this incredible turquoisey blue-green, like you'd see on a cloisonné vase, and paint it on the reverse side of glass. Then use it as a tabletop. You have the effect of color, once removed — even the most color-phobic will usually go for it. And it looks so glossy and deep. Absolutely ravishing."

ELISSA CULLMAN

BENJAMIN MOORE | SILKEN PINE 2144-50

"Pale green is a kind of universal donor. Even our most beige clients seem to respond well to green, probably because it's a color we see so much in nature. This is a soft, celadony green, like a piece of the palest jade. I'll often use it in a master bedroom."

ANTONIO DA MOTTA

DONALD KAUFMAN COLOR COLLECTION | DKC-17

"A hallway tends to be a dead space, but paint it this warm Etruscan red and it's a blast of life. You don't have to live in it. You're just walking through. But it's a hook. People can get addicted to color after they paint a hallway."

Wainscoting and woodwork painted in a light white set off the blue-gray walls of this entry hall and stairway wall, designed by Madeline Stuart.

MADELINE STUART
FARROW & BALL | LIGHT BLUE 22

"I'm always surprised when clients balk at color and never surprised when they realize the difference it makes. In a transitional space like a stair hall, you have more freedom, so we tried a grayish modified blue—soft, but with great depth. Once the client saw how it enriched the space, the deal was done."

OPPOSITE PAGE :

"After we bought the place we were flying up from Florida to Atlanta, and as we came through the clouds I said, "This is what I want to wake up to every morning, a feeling of lightness and airiness, like we're floating on a meringue." Polished woods and shots of gold—the gilt of a picture frame, the dull brass of a chandelier—warm the palette up and bring it to life."

PHOEBE HOWARD FARROW & BALL | CLUNCH 2009

CHERYL KATZ
BENJAMIN MOORE | COASTAL FOG AC-1

"This is a color for people who think they want all white. It's a warm gray with a little hint of green—a good choice for a living room since it still lets you have a neutral envelope, but it's not boring. Cool it down with icy blues, or warm it up with mustard."

SCOTT SANDERS
BENJAMIN MOORE | CORAL REEF 012

"Don't give guests a white room—they probably have that at home. Take a chance on this bright coral, softer than orange and more hip than pink. Very Palm Beach and lobster salad on a summer day."

BARRY DIXON

FARROW & BALL
| PICTURE GALLERY RED 42 (LEFT)
| FOWLER PINK 39 (RIGHT)

"I took the color of a seashell—actually, it was the inside lip of a conch where it goes into this rosy, fleshy tone—and then re-created it with three parts **Picture Gallery Red** to one part **Fowler Pink.** If you can find the color somewhere in nature, it often makes people feel more comfortable."

KATHRYN M. IRELAND

FARROW & BALL | BORROWED LIGHT 235

"Start with something pale. Then add more color, if you like, with fabric. This is a beautiful, restful blue, very soft on the eye. Lends itself particularly well to antiques and faded fabrics."

KEITH IRVINE

BENJAMIN MOORE | UTAH SKY 2065-40

"It's a clean, simple jolt of blue. Simple, like all good American traditions, and I would use it in an entrance hall, against a clear white trim. The next injection of color will be a hell of a lot easier."

SUZANNE LOVELL

DONALD KAUFMAN COLOR COLLECTION | DKC-66

"I'd go straight to the library and paint it this deep, luscious purplish brown, like the bark of a tree when it's wet in the rain. A dark color actually expands the space, because it erases the boundaries. Then the room becomes all about the books and the art."

TODD KLEIN

BENJAMIN MOORE | MAN ON THE MOON OC-106

"The client wanted yellow in the living room but was afraid to commit, so we landed on this wonderful warm cream, the color of a magnolia petal. As the day wanes, it gets deeper and really starts to glow once the lights are turned on. Who doesn't need a little moonglow in their life?"

NOEL JEFFREY

BENJAMIN MOORE | MORNING GLORY 785

"Do this soft blue in a bedroom, and it would be like waking up to a clear bright morning. If the person is really nervous about color, paint all the trim white. Do white furniture, white fabrics, white bed linens—then you can have a blue room without hitting them over the head with it."

The ceiling was glazed in a custom off-white
with a touch of gold to pick up on the glint of
all the acting awards.

TRIED AND TRUE CLASSICS

We called interior decorators with long, distinguished careers and asked: What "classic" palettes do you always come back to? Their answers may surprise you.

"I'm mad about this dark inky blue, as it gives great vibrancy and depth to a wall—especially if you put a topcoat of good clear varnish over it. That's what we did in Rex Harrison's Manhattan apartment in this fabulous little dining alcove. You can almost see yourself reflected in it."

KEITH IRVINE
BENJAMIN MOORE | DARK ROYAL BLUE 2065-20

ROSE TARLOW

FARROW & BALL | ALL WHITE 2005 (TOP)

| POINTING 2003 (CENTER)

| SLIPPER SATIN 2004 (BOTTOM)

"I never paint every wall in a room the same color. Light hits each wall in a different way, so I have to adjust the shade. It's usually white, but not one white. All White is a pure white, Pointing has a little ocher, and Slipper Satin has more gray. One of the most important things is how the shadows fall. That can be the most beautiful of all."

JOHN SALADINO

BENJAMIN MOORE | ORIENTAL IRIS 1418

"I'm emotionally attracted to periwinkle blue. It goes from gray into blue into lavender, depending on the time of day and month of year and the person looking at it. Blue combines two things I love, the ocean and the sky, which lifts me out of the quagmire of reality. It's a kind of bath. It represents a cleansing."

The walls in this master bedroom, designed by Phoebe Howard are painted in Farrow & Ball's Slipper Satin 2004.

DAVID EASTON

PAPERS & PAINTS LTD. | MOORISH RED HC55

"You can see the ground-up pigment in this paint, which gives it depth and a little iridescence. It's not flat, like American paints. It conjures up Greek vases and the walls of Knossos. It has the weight of antiquity."

BARBARA WESTBROOK

DONALD KAUFMAN COLOR COLLECTION | DKC-5

"It's a small bathroom, so I wanted everything built-in, precise, and neat. And yet it turned out charming and inviting. You wouldn't believe the number of people who pass through it and say they're dying to get into that bathtub."

BETTY SHERRILL

FARROW & BALL | MINSTER GREEN 224

"Green is my favorite color. It's just so soothing, and I think a library should be a soothing dark color. Wood, if you can have it. If you can't, make it this woodsy green. I like it glazed. I think any paint color is better glazed—it has more depth."

WILLIAM HODGINS

BENJAMIN MOORE | DECK ENAMEL RICH BROWN 60 (TOP)

| DECK ENAMEL BLACK C-112-80

(BOTTOM)

"It's a great formula—rich brown mixed half and half with black. Decorating people call this *tête de negre*, but that's so highfalutin'. It's just a beautiful dark brown with some gloss to it. Try it with white trim and a touch of pink."

CHARLOTTE MOSS

FARROW & BALL | VERT DE TERRE 234

"This is the furry, fuzzy green of lamb's ears. Very herbal. It's rich without being too saturated, and makes a great backdrop for mahogany, silver, or ivory. It's the color of my fantasy room—a book-lined great ballroom with a lit Polonaise in the middle of the limestone floor and orange trees in tubs. A pavilion in the forest."

VICENTE WOLF

BENJAMIN MOORE | PATRIOTIC WHITE 2135-70

"When the sun streams in, the walls read white, and then, as the day progresses, the color comes out. At night, the room is bathed in a pale, pale blue-green. I love the mercurial quality of it. It looks beautiful by the ocean, because it echoes the subtleties of the sea."

SALLY SIRKIN LEWIS

BENJAMIN MOORE | SMOKEY TAUPE 983

"This is the color of a beautiful Belgian linen. Very classic. Not too light and not too dark, but with enough depth to look great on a wall. Natural materials like limestone and granite look great against it. Bring in black lacquer, white upholstery, and red for an accent."

MARIO BUATTA

BENJAMIN MOORE | SUNDANCE 2022-50

"This is a medium-strength yellow, the color of fresh pineapple. People love it. It's just a happy color. Try it in a living room or dining room with a pale blue ceiling and white woodwork. It's like sunshine. Everything looks good against it—blue-and-white porcelain, a floral chintz."

FARROW & BALL | MATCHSTICK 2013

A pair of old rounded corbels from a church ceiling were turned into wall anchors for these elegant canopy beds. Two coats of a bright white high-gloss paint gave them a dramatic effect against the warmly evocative Matchstick, by Farrow & Ball.

Crisp white walls balance dark-wood
furnishings in a room designed by
Betsy Brown, who strives to create
"a harmony of opposites."

WHICH WHITE IS THE BEST WHITE?

It's the ideal backdrop for fine art, an appropriate emphasis for architecture, and a noncompetitive companion for all other color. No wonder we love white: It brings the best qualities of every room to light.

"I love color, but I think it should either declare itself the major player in a composition or quietly add the crucial notes that balance a room and make it intriguing. I usually opt for the latter."

BETSY BROWN
PRATT & LAMBERT | SILVER LINING 32-32

"It's the classic formula. Linen White looks as if it's been on the wall a long time, which works very well with old English and French furniture. But it can be a little too yellow, so I usually cool it down with Decorators White to make something a bit lighter and more sophisticated."

KEITH IRVINE

BENJAMIN MOORE | LINEN WHITE INTERIOR ROOM
MIXED WITH
| DECORATOR'S WHITE INT. RM.

PETER PENNOYER

FARROW & BALL | STRONG WHITE 2001

"If you have a wall with a bow in it or a floor that has settled, this will make an old room feel graceful rather than brand new. It has more pigment and therefore more character."

JEROME NEUNER

BENJAMIN MOORE | SUPER WHITE INTERIOR ROOM

"After testing every conceivable white and even mixing some ourselves, we wound up using this off-the-shelf paint in the galleries of the Museum of Modern Art. It's bright and clean, yet still has a little warmth to it."

ALEXA HAMPTON

BENJAMIN MOORE | IVORY WHITE 925

"This color looks great everywhere. It's a creamy, buttery white that my father (decorator Mark Hampton) liked to use, but I'm even more obsessive about it. Try an eggshell finish on the walls to reflect light but not look too glossy."

MARIETTE HIMES GOMEZ

DONALD KAUFMAN COLOR COLLECTION | DKC-51

"You can see every color in it—it's a chameleon that changes with natural light. Anything you put near it is comfortable. This white is going to be with me for the rest of my life."

MURRAY MOSS

BENJAMIN MOORE | SUPER WHITE INTERIOR ROOM

"Everything looks good against a true, clear, eye-chilling, freezing-cold white. It's like a blizzard, or Ascot, or Huck Finn's white fence, or marshmallows, or sugar. Anything placed against that background projects like Technicolor."

THOMAS JAYNE

BENJAMIN MOORE | ACADIA WHITE OC-38

"It has a nice green cast to it; perfect for a summer house in a leafy setting. It acts as a bridge to the outdoors."

CRAIG SCHUMACHER AND PHILIP KIRK
BEHR PAINTS | PLANTATION WHITE WN-18

Craig and Phillip painted the beadboard walls and ceiling of this bedroom a warm white, creating an effective "gallery" for a collection of paintings, drawings, prints, and photographs. The white gives the walls a lovely rustic sort of whitewash feel.

JUSTINE CUSHING
BENJAMIN MOORE | DECORATOR'S WHITE
INTERIOR ROOM

Justine Cushing designed this cozy country cottage in her trademark chintz. She had the living room walls painted **Decorator's White** by **Benjamin Moore** because of the low ceilings.

RICHARD GLUCKMAN
BENJAMIN MOORE | CHINA WHITE INTERIOR ROOM

"You don't want a highly reflective wall surface if you're going to be hanging a lot of art. China White is a very subtle off-white with a gray tone that helps the work stand out."

JONATHAN ADLER
RALPH LAUREN PAINT | POCKET WATCH WHITE WW11

"When it comes to whites I use only Pocket Watch White. It's soft and warm but not cream, and still undeniably white. It will make a room look gracious and young at the same time."

KELLY WEARSTLER
PRATT & LAMBERT | SEED PEARL 27-32

"I put it on every ceiling in my house. It's a clean, crisp white that has a little bit of warmth in it, which gives it more depth and dimension. I use it on moldings for contrast."

THOMAS PHEASANT
BENJAMIN MOORE | IVORY WHITE 925

"It's tough to get a crisp look without being cold. Ivory White does the trick. It's the most flexible white I've come across and works with any color. Carry it from room to room on the trim."

In a sleek Manhattan apartment, the living room
walls are bathed in **Bella Donna**, a smoky lavender
neutral with both refinement and sex appeal.

SOOTHING
NEUTRALS

Neutrals are the starting point for almost any palette. But which neutrals? You can't go wrong making a commitment to a color that you love. Colors with a little zing go with everything.

"I've been using Bella Donna a lot. It's a smoky lavender gray, the color of a twilight sky. I used it on the parlor floor of a brownstone, and it looked flat-out sophisticated. I'm in the bedroom of my country house right now, which is painted this color. Bella Donna is a sexy, adult color, but it can go a lot of different ways."

DD ALLEN C2, BELLA DONNA | C2-316 W

CHRISTOPHER MAYA

BENJAMIN MOORE | GLASS SLIPPER 1632

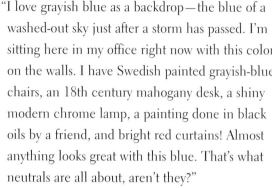

"I love grayish blue as a backdrop—the blue of a washed-out sky just after a storm has passed. I'm sitting here in my office right now with this color on the walls. I have Swedish painted grayish-blue chairs, an 18th century mahogany desk, a shiny modern chrome lamp, a painting done in black oils by a friend, and bright red curtains! Almost anything looks great with this blue. That's what neutrals are all about, aren't they?"

JENNIFER GARRIGUES

BENJAMIN MOORE | MESQUITE 501

"Mesquite is a flattering light moss green without much yellow. I love it because it doesn't shout 'I'm green!' It says, 'I'm a very beautiful color.'"

MATTHEW PATRICK SMYTH

BENJAMIN MOORE | LINEN WHITE 70

"When in doubt, Linen White: You can phone that in. It might seem like a cop-out, but it works beautifully. I use it when people are unsure. They want something light and airy but not stark white. No matter what light you put it in, it looks good."

KEN FULK
PHILIP'S PERFECT COLOR
| AGUA VERTE PPC-BL7 (LEFT)
| MINK PPC-G13 (RIGHT)

"The walls are a taupey brown.
They're pretty rich. The Mink gives
oomph and weight to live up to the
architecture of the room, and the pale
blue, which I've also used in the
backs of the bookcases, makes it a
little more playful and vaporous."

MICHAEL SMITH
PRATT & LAMBERT | SILVER BLOND 14-29
Michael painted the cabinets and trim a soft buttermilk to use
the natural sunlight to add light and space to the room and
give it a vintage feel. It also allows the colorful furnishings—
the antique Chinese lanterns, the blue-washed table and
chair, the warm stone countertop—to really pop.

CHRISTOPHER RIDOLFI

BENJAMIN MOORE | GRANT BEIGE HC-83

"My standby is Grant Beige. It's like a favorite pair of worn khakis. It fares equally well with the light of Texas or the East Coast."

MARY MCDONALD

DUNN-EDWARDS | COCONUT SKIN DE1055

"I could paint every room in the house Coconut Skin, a deep mocha brown with some milk in it. It's cozy and comforting without being kidsy: grounding with pastels, weighty with bright colors."

MARIETTE HIMES GOMEZ

FARROW & BALL | STRING 8 (TOP)
        | GREEN GROUND 206 (BOTTOM)

"Khaki and celadon are my picks. These are colors, but they're still very neutral in their integrity. Each one is softly beautiful. They don't scream. They don't dictate—you can put them with anything."

STEVEN GAMBREL

BENJAMIN MOORE | HORIZON 1478

"I always come back to Horizon, a pale gray that doesn't turn blue or green on you. It's a sophisticated background to so many interiors. Blues look beautiful against this gray, but so do pinks and lavenders."

GERRIE BREMERMANN

BENJAMIN MOORE | PAPAYA 957

"The most enduring color I've found looks like homemade vanilla ice cream with a little caramel in it. I love it with the blues, greens, and blue-greens of the sea and sky, and with various soft warm pinks. There's nothing edgy about it, which suits me fine."

Kathy used autumn colors—brown, beige, and gold neutrals with a splash of coral—to give this living room depth and warmth. When you walk in, you feel instantly enveloped and safe.

KATHY SMITH FARROW & BALL | BISCUIT 38

ELLEN KENNON

FULL SPECTRUM PAINTS | MUSHROOM

"Mushroom changes drastically—one minute putty and the next, rosier. Chameleon-like and mysterious, it takes on the properties of the colors around it."

JEFFREY BILHUBER

BENJAMIN MOORE | PALE VISTA 2029-60

"I use spring green as a neutral. It's the color of buds and bulbs popping out of the ground after a long winter—a reassuring color, great in a bedroom."

MALLORY MARSHALL

BENJAMIN MOORE | WENGE AF-180

"Wenge is the color of bitter chocolate with 70% cacao that everyone's calling health food. A neutral should get along with every color in the fan deck, and this one is like the nicest girl in the sixth grade."

SUSAN FERRIER
BENJAMIN MOORE
DANVILLE TAN HC-91
"I think it's very important to limit color, to be restrained. I look for colors with good vibrations to create harmony with the eye. Here I used blue-grays, green-blues, and brown-greens. Every single color is hard to put your finger on."

JEFFREY BILHUBER
BENJAMIN MOORE | PEACE AND HAPPINESS 1380
"Lavender is the new beige. From lilac to amethyst, it's an extraordinary neutral and a great unifier—a soothing, peaceful color that is timeless."

DARRYL CARTER
BENJAMIN MOORE | LOOKOUT POINT 1646
"It's one of those elusive non-colors that reminds me of the time between morning dew and sunrise—a perfect marriage between pale blue. Whatever room you put it in, it creates a calm, serene mood."

STEVEN GAMBREL

BENJAMIN MOORE | SEA STAR 2123-30

"I like very pale teal. It's a nice background for highly textured washed-out beige textiles, and together they make a kind of faded beach story, pulling together the greens of the earth, the grays of the sky, and the blue-greens of the water."

KEN FULK

PHILIP'S PERFECT COLORS | ADOBE 08

"I'll be stoned for saying terra-cotta—but I have one really excellent color. The beautiful thing about it is that it is earthen and Old Worldy, but it can work in a modern setting, and it looks great with really dark floors or pale, washed-out oak."

MARY MCDONALD

BENJAMIN MOORE | ROMANTIC PINK 2004-70

"Anywhere you're going to use white, consider pastel pink instead—for walls, ceilings, furniture, and lampshades. Then paint your floors pastel pink! You can't believe how many colors look great with it. What people don't realize is that you can also make it masculine by adding deep, rich saturated hues to your color scheme—chocolate brown, dark gray, navy, or eggplant."

GERRIE BREMERMANN

BENJAMIN MOORE | RACCOON HOLLOW 978

"We just got back from France, where I couldn't help noticing that everything is painted what I call Avignon taupe—that flaxy natural color that's a little on the gray side."

JENNIFER GARRIGUES

SHERWIN-WILLIAMS | HONIED WHITE 7106

"It looks like white with sunlight in it. You can use it with saturated colors or the airiest whites and creams, and it works no matter what the light is, it never turns funny colors."

JACK YOUNG

BENJAMIN MOORE | CORAL SPICE 2170-40

"In the intense light of Palm Beach, real colors make great neutrals, but colors that are quieted down. I like pale coral for a living room. It looks great with aqua, rattan, and bamboo."

NANCY BRAITHWAITE

BENJAMIN MOORE | VAN BUREN BROWN HC-70

"Chocolate brown settles a room and receives creams, reds, yellows, and blues beautifully. If you have insipid architecture, you should definitely consider it because walls fade away."

A vaulted ceiling, alcove windows, and an unusual yellow give this master bedroom a sense of airiness and drama.

MADELINE STUART
FARROW & BALL | PALE HOUND 71

"It's one of the most fabulously odd colors. It's a slightly bilious yellow, not the easiest color, but it has such depth and nuance. Juxtaposed against the James White trim, it's so crisp and unexpected. I adore this color."

SARA BENGUR

DONALD KAUFMAN COLOR COLLECTION | DKC-20

"Ocher feels like a neutral to me—a deep, earthy yellow that reminds me of southern Italy and Turkey. It looks good with other earthy colors, like terra-cotta or gray-blue, and it is really beautiful with lilac, lime green, and aubergine. People look at it and say, "Oh no, I couldn't possibly." But the earthier colors can be really relaxing."

RICHARD GLUCKMAN

BENJAMIN MOORE | BEAR CREEK 1470

"This mysterious, warm sort of aubergine is great for painting exposed steel structural elements. I got it directly from the painter Francesco Clemente's studio. All the doors, window frames, railings, and steel structure are painted Bear Creek, with a concrete floor and pale green cement board walls—very beautiful."

VICENTE WOLF

BENJAMIN MOORE | GRAYTINT 1611

"I love pearl gray for a foyer, bedroom, or hallway—anywhere you want a sense of intimacy. If there's a big white space with a niche, I would paint only the niche this soft gray. I always like shadowy, mercurial colors that play up the mysteries of architecture."

PHOEBE HOWARD
FARROW & BALL
SHADED WHITE 201
Phoebe painted her dining room walls a dark off-white, both unobtrusive and mellow, but kept it bright enough to make the best use of the natural light available.

BARBARA BARRY
DONALD KAUFMAN COLOR COLLECTION | DKC-8

"Green is the great neutral, all the way from pond scum to soft sage or pale celery. I recently moved into a new house surrounded by greenery, and when I was thinking of what color I might use for a drapery lining, it came to me to reflect the green that is present year-round right outside that window."

MALLORY MARSHALL

SHERWIN-WILLIAMS | DETERMINED ORANGE 6635

"Orange is a wonderful neutral. It can't be a washed-out orange—it has to be a color you'd want to lick, which is why the good oranges are always called Salsa or Punch. You have to be just a little bit afraid of your orange."

SUSAN FERRIER

FARROW & BALL | LIGHT BLUE 22

"It works well for bedrooms, bathrooms, and especially work spaces, because it's a powerful yet gentle mediator, bringing calm to all that clutter."

DD ALLEN

C2 | SORCERER 5326

"I recently did a dining room with these dark blue-berry walls, a chocolate brown rug, gold curtains, a mahogany table, and chairs upholstered in burgundy. Navy makes a great, sexy evening room—after all, it's the color of night."

CHRISTOPHER RIDOLFI

FARROW & BALL | COOKING APPLE GREEN 32

"It has gray in it, but there's still brightness within. To me it looks great with all metal finishes—bronze, wrought iron, nickel."

KATHY SMITH

SHERWIN-WILLIAMS | PALE EARTH 8133

Kathy chose a subtle creamy beige for this master bathroom. It becomes vibrant when bathed in sunlight, exuding warmth and elegance with a very European kind of sophistication.

RUTHIE SOMMERS
BENJAMIN MOORE
ICEBERG 2122-50
"That unexpected bright blue is what made me fall in love with the house. It was such a great palette to start with. The natural inclination is to go pale—but the darker colors add punch. This is a house that screams, 'I'm at the beach! Relax!'"

SHARONE EINHORN AND HONEY WOLTERS
BENJAMIN MOORE | NOVEMBER RAIN 2142-60

"We just finished decorating a bungalow where we struggled picking paint colors because the owner had just stripped all the wood trim and didn't want to paint it. All the colors we picked changed totally in the presence of that orangey—light brown wood. A contractor finally told us about Benjamin Moore's November Rain—it's a putty color, warm but not too warm, and it looked great everywhere we put it."

MYRA HOEFER
FARROW & BALL | DOWN PIPE 26

"It's charcoal, but I think of it as wet stone, wet cement, or even soot. It's a fabulous color for trim—they use it in French and English houses all the time. In a kitchen, if you paint the walls and cabinets this color and use a lot of mirrors, you'd have a very rich, town housey, sexy alternative to the all-white kitchen."

ELLEN KENNON
FULL SPECTRUM PAINTS | BUTTERCREAM

"Buttercream is my favorite unexpected neutral. It's innately uplifting because it's the color of sunshine— an antidepressant with no side effects! But very pale yellow also soothes and looks great with rich, dark woods, blues, and greens. There's not a single color that doesn't work with it."

STEPHEN SILLS
BENJAMIN MOORE | STONE HARBOR 2111-50

"Any color can be a neutral if it is grayed off with a touch of black and used all over a room, without any other color interrupting it. I particularly love greens as neutrals: moss, sage, stone, hunter. I like to use many different tones."

FAYE CONE
DONALD KAUFMAN COLOR COLLECTION | DKC

Faye chose a reflective neutral that echoes the res
bedroom. Here, pale ivory walls give the illusion of
space without taking away from the natural beauty
whitewashed bed frame.

AMELIA HANDEGAN

FINE PAINTS OF EUROPE | LP-16

"Butterscotch makes a nice burnished backdrop. It changes with the light—it can look like wheat or like a darker buff with an orange tone. At night it seems candlelit."

GARY MCBOURNIE

BENJAMIN MOORE | RED PARROT 1308

"Red has always been a neutral for me. I like it somewhere between claret and fire engine, so it's really red but with a slight bit of brown to it. It's cozy, glowing, and sexy."

TOM SCHEERER

PRATT & LAMBERT | DEEP JUNGLE 21-17

"I've always used what I call gardenia-leaf green. Put it on the walls and then bounce two other colors off it, like sky blue and coral pink. Fresh greens end up in virtually every room I put together."

MATTHEW PATRICK SMYTH

BENJAMIN MOORE | WICKHAM GRAY HC-171

"Lately I've been using a whole series of grays, every-thing from steel to a warm French gray. You want to be careful when picking your gray—nothing too sad, cold, or dingy."

CHEERFUL **BLUES**

Elegant and ethereal. Deep and mysterious. Cool and icy. Bright and breezy. Cerulean blue, azure blue, robin's egg blue, indigo blue, sapphire blue. Every blue has a mood and a personality. Every blue tells a story. Which blue tells your story?

The tiny guest room is the only room in David's house given a deep wall color, a modern spin on the classic blue-and-white bedroom. It gives the space a distinctly masculine feel.

DAVID JIMENEZ
BENJAMIN MOORE | STARRY NIGHT BLUE 2067-20

RALPH HARVARD

SHERWIN-WILLIAMS/ DURON, COLORS OF HISTORIC
CHARLESTON | VERDITER BLUE, DCR078 NRH

"This is an intense 18th-century blue-green. They used to make it by pouring acids on copper and using the verdigris as the pigment for the paint."

WHITNEY STEWART

C2 | ELECTRIC 275

"What you want is an evening blue, an Yves Klein blue. It's contemplative, meditative, mysterious. When I want to be enveloped, blue is the only color that will do it for me."

WILLIAM DIAMOND AND ANTHONY BARATTA

SHERWIN-WILLIAMS | SASSY BLUE 1241

"Blue is my secret-agent color. I'm always sneaking it in these days. I guess it's like a bit of sky peeking out."

ERIC COHLER

FARROW & BALL | CHINESE BLUE 90

"This is not too hot, not too cold, with a lot of green, which makes it feel grounded. Blue is so regenerative. There's the idea of water, renewal. It's powerful, regal—bluebloods, blue ribbons."

The turquoise on the walls looks even richer next to woodwork painted Benjamin Moore's Ivory White 925 (page 33) in the corner of this dining room by Markham Roberts.

MARKHAM ROBERTS
PARKER PAINT | WATERSIDE 7573M

"This bright, pretty turquoise reminds me of summers on Lake Michigan when I was a child, skipping stones and looking up at the sky, and feeling the sun on my body. Blue calms me and reenergizes me—just as the ocean does."

The unexpected swimming pool blue in this entryway makes Ruthie Sommers' client fall in love with the whole house. It's a blue that evokes the spirit of the sea in this quintessential summer cottage.

RUTHIE SOMMERS

BENJAMIN MOORE | BLUE SEAFOAM 2056-60

JOHN YUNIS

BENJAMIN MOORE | AQUARIUS 788

"I've never met a blue I didn't like. Everything from the darkest to the lightest—and this is in the middle—with a hint of aquamarine."

ROGER DE CABROL

BENJAMIN MOORE | PATRIOT BLUE 2064-20

"I don't like baby blue or sky blue—I like dark, strong cobalt blue. It reminds me of Europe, in the sense of luxuriousness and the privacy it creates in a room. It shields you."

THOMAS JAYNE

BENJAMIN MOORE | HEAVENLY BLUE 709

"This is the color of the sky in Old Master paintings, when the varnish has yellowed; it's luminous. Paint just the floor—you'd feel as if you were floating."

JAMIE DRAKE
BENJAMIN MOORE | WINDMILL WINGS 2067-60

"Blue is America's favorite color. It's certainly the most telegenic. That's why politicians wear blue shirts and why the new White House pressroom is blue. It's cool. It's calming. This is an ethereal blue, with a touch of red that gives it a lavender cast."

DAVID KLEINBERG
BENJAMIN MOORE | COLONY GREEN 694

"I grew up in a house that was all turquoise, and for years I couldn't look at blue. But this color is so terrifically pretty and filled with joy—sort of like as if you were inside a robin's egg looking out into the light. I'd use it in a bedroom with white lacquered trim, a four-poster bed lacquered white, and crisp white bed linens."

ROBIN BELL
BENJAMIN MOORE | PADDINGTON BLUE 791

"This is a peacock blue, a very happy, exuberant blue that would set off all the objects in a room. I'd use it in a high-gloss finish with lots of white moldings. Blue is one of the best colors around for crispness and contrast. After all, what looks better than a naval officer in his dress blues?"

PHOEBE HOWARD
SHERWIN-WILLIAMS
BLUE HUBBARD 8438
"I just gravitate toward the softer blues and greens and sand colors. My client brought me a Jim Thompson silk ad that had all these bright blues and greens in it—cobalt, turquoise, lime, jade. She said, 'These colors. Take this with you.'"

ELISSA CULLMAN

BENJAMIN MOORE | BLUE WAVE 2065-50

"Blue is tricky. It can go gray and sad. But not this warm Mediterranean blue. It's the blue in all those Pucci prints, a bright, happy, not-a-cloud-in-the-sky blue, as if you're in vacation mode and having lobster and rosé at Tetou on the beach near Cannes. I love it in a bedroom, where you could crisp it up with a navy-and-white-striped fabric and one of those great Elizabeth Eakins plaid rugs."

In a Palm Beach entrance hall, designed by Lee
Beirly and Christopher Drake, saturated yellow
is set off by moldings painted with Benjamin
Moore White Dove semi-gloss enamel.

ENTERING THE HOME

It's the first space you see when you arrive home and the place where your guests form their first impression. If you want it to be inviting, color is the answer.

"It's one of those spaces that people go through quickly, so you can afford a higher level of drama. Often, there's no natural light, so you need a heavily saturated color like this warm, yolky yellow. Get it in full gloss because the gloss gives it depth, and it's much simpler to apply than glazing."

CHRISTOPHER DRAKE
BENJAMIN MOORE | SHOWTIME 923

ROBERT GOODWIN
BENJAMIN MOORE | IRON MOUNTAIN 2134-30
Goodwin painted the trim the same dark blue-brown as
the walls to give it a modern spin. Everything in this
eclectic entryway is surprising: the rich taupe, the French
console, the English mirror, the Chinese porcelain, the
crazily gilt brackets.

KEITH IRVINE

BENJAMIN MOORE | SALSA 2009-20

"Red is the color of excitement, and I tend to go for corally orange reds. With red, you know you've arrived and you glance in the mirror and realize how great you look and breeze right in."

EVE ROBINSON

FARROW & BALL | DRAB 41

"I like a progression of color. It's good to start dark—this is so moody and has a wonderful earthy tone—and as you move inside, the rooms become lighter, which makes them seem more spacious."

JOHN OETGEN

BENJAMIN MOORE | PALLADIAN BLUE HC-144

"If you took green and sky blue and put them in a bucket with a lot of air, this is what you would get. I even put it on the ceiling. It looks great with black-and-white floors. I'd add a bronze bench with shocking pink upholstery."

PATRICIA HEALING

FINE PAINTS OF EUROPE | DUTCH CHOCOLATE 6012

"Imagine you're melting dark chocolate in a saucepan—that's the color. It glistens. This high-gloss paint looks almost like patent leather."

SUZANNE KASLER
BENJAMIN MOORE | ELEPHANT TUSK OC-8

With this project, the designer kept the whole house very tone on tone, with naturals, camels, tans, and browns. Here a clean ivory color allows the sculptural faux-bois balustrade and hand-colored engravings to really stand out.

T. KELLER DONOVAN
BENJAMIN MOORE | LINEN WHITE 70

"A hall takes such a beating. Mine looks like the shipping department at Macy's. So I'd choose a cool, calm white. Fill a mayonnaise jar with it and keep it in the closet for touch-ups."

....

JOHN BARMAN
RALPH LAUREN PAINT | RACER PINK 1B07

"It's a strong, vibrant pink, as masculine as you can get in a pink, with a nice shine to it. In a small entrance hall, I like to use deep strong colors to help define the space. Otherwise, you lose it."

....

STEVEN GAMBREL
PRATT & LAMBERT | ARGENT 1322

"Those 18th-century British architects kept the front hallway somber to recall the color of the stone outside, on the façade. I like the idea of bringing the outside in, but stone doesn't necessarily work for me. I tend to use a sky-bluish color that has a pretty heavy dose of gray and green."

OPPOSITE PAGE :

An unexpected splash of bright lavender along the staircase wall sets a playful mood in the entry hall of this stone cottage designed by Eldon Wong.

ELDON WONG

BEHR'S DISNEY HOME CLASSIC POOH | BUTTERFLY FLUTTER BY DC2A-10-1

JENNIFER GARRIGUES

FARROW & BALL | FOLLY GREEN 76

"Imagine going down a leafy path and opening the door to a lovely green foyer. This is not the usual dark bottle green. It's paler and softer, a really good go-anywhere green that feels very peaceful."

WHITNEY STEWART

C2 | QUAHOG 8385

"You want to make wow! but at the same time, you have to be neutral because it's the opener for the rest of the apartment. So what to do? Paint your hall this fabulous gray-taupe, which is still neutral but dark enough to make a statement."

T. KELLER DONOVAN
BENJAMIN MOORE | SUMMER SHOWER 2135-60
"A blue-and-white scheme brightens a room with no
natural light. I chose Summer Shower because it has the
coolness of the blue deep within a chunk of ice. Benjamin
Moore's White Dove makes trim look tailored and crisp."

HERMES MALLEA

DONALD KAUFMAN COLOR COLLECTION | DKC-17

"We painted this tight little space an intense barn red. Everything around you was red—walls, ceilings, doors. You were completely encapsulated in red, so you couldn't really tell the dimensions."

KERRY JOYCE

SHERWIN-WILLIAMS | STUDIO MAUVE 0062

"This is a velvety gray with just the right amount of lavender. If it had any more lavender in it, it would be well beyond my pain threshold, but it doesn't, so it's perfect."

WILLIAM EUBANKS

BENJAMIN MOORE | GOLDEN STRAW 2152-50

"I'm attracted to warm colors that kind of wrap their arms around you. This is like candlelight, with a wonderful golden glow. I'll put layers of glaze over it so it's as rich in daytime as it is at night."

TOM BRITT

FINE PAINTS OF EUROPE | SPINNAKER WHITE 7032

"Right now, we're into this traditional oil paint in a color that looks like whipped cream. Get it in the Brilliant finish and it's very shiny, like gelato. Seriously, make your entry refreshing. Cool off."

RELAXING **IN THE LIVING ROOM**

Looking to match your living room to your personality? From passionate reds to muted neutrals, bold blues to sensual browns, get your inspiration from the examples on these pages.

"Coral and sunflower yellow is a palette I've used before. A monochromatic beige scheme would not have taken this house anywhere. I used a personal fabric I developed. It's a fancy print by Quadrille, but I had them run it for me on orange and white mattress ticking to countrify it."

TOM SHEERER

BENJAMIN MOORE | MORNING SUNSHINE 2018-50

AMANDA KYSER
BENJAMIN MOORE | ONYX 2133-10
Here's a nice trick from designer Amanda Kyser: If you
have a very large, open living room, you can divide the
space up visually using a very dark contrasting color on
the windows, baseboards and trim. This dark onyx helps to
define the windows without making them gloomy.

JOE NYE

BENJAMIN MOORE | SHENANDOAH TAUPE AC-36

The cocoa brown color of this study is a dramatic depar-
ture from the rest of the house. Joe Nye wanted to give his
client one masculine, subdued room for a change of pace.
The room doubles as a guest bedroom and office, so the
quiet color is perfect.

JASON BELL

BENJAMIN MOORE
  | SADDLE SOAP 2110-30
  | TUDOR BROWN
  | LADYBUG RED 1322

Jason Bell chose a dark olive for the walls, paired with a very rich brown on the trim and bookcases, for this non-traditional English country house. To add a hint of color, the back interiors of the bookshelves are painted a cheerful ladybug red, which nicely complements the red in the chair and sofa. It's cozy without being somber.

MYRA HOEFER

BENJAMIN MOORE | HORIZON GRAY 2141-50

"In this living room, there are many elegant things, lots of silks and textured velvets, but the wall color creates such a delicate, soft mood. I call it a non-color. It's like being inside a beautiful egg. You don't really know if it's a powder blue or a gray or a pale olive, but it's a color from nature, and it puts you at peace."

MARY McDONALD
BENJAMIN MOORE | LAVENDER ICE 2069-60

"I knew I wanted to bring green in here as an accent. But we wanted it more subtle and calming. I found a romantic, feminine, flowery Lee Jofa cotton print, which I put on a pair of slipper chairs I designed. The print has moss green washed-out chartreuse and a little bit of lavender gray in it. I pulled the lavender gray wall color from that."

RON WOODSON AND JAIME RUMMERFIELD
SHERWIN-WILLIAMS | LEAPFROG 6431
"You have to listen to what the house is asking for. For us,
the blue and green combo is all about the beach. I think
color can't be halfway or 'Hmmmm, should I?' It's all or
nothing for us. There has to be a twist, something that's
almost not natural to the combination."

This kitchen was set up primarily for entertaining,
with the big blond-wood center table as a buffet.

ENTERTAINING KITCHEN WALLS

When you're ready to break away from the classic white kitchen, where will you turn? Try these clean, fresh, and inviting alternatives.

The deep olive green color on the built-in millwork and cabinets was perfect. Chad Eisner chose this color to add depth to show off the blond-wood center table.

CHAD EISNER
PRATT & LAMBERT | FLINT 32-20

CLARE DONOHUE
BENJAMIN MOORE | WEDGEWOOD GRAY HC-146 (TOP)
| WOODLAWN BLUE HC-147 (BOTTOM)
"Wedgewood Gray and Woodlawn Blue have that robin's egg
vibe. I always hedge my bets toward grayed-down shades,
because bright colors that look so happy in the paint store
can look bizarre in real life. If you're nervous, start by painting the back wall inside the cabinets."

PAULA PERLINI

BENJAMIN MOORE | WARM SIENNA 1203

"Might as well make it cozy. Everybody comes in anyway—you can't beat them out with a spoon. Plates would look great on the wall against this warm cayenne, and I'd do teak countertops and cork on the floor—very soft and warm to bare feet."

BEVERLY ELLSLEY

BENJAMIN MOORE | GOLDEN HONEY 297

"Kitchens often have so little wall space you have to make the color count. This is sunshine in a can. I like a yellow with a little bit of brown in it, as opposed to a yellow with green. Looks wonderful with wood."

JOANNE HUDSON

SHERWIN-WILLIAMS | WHOLE WHEAT SW6121

"It's the color of golden brown sugar. Very appetizing, with a lot of warmth. I'd use it on the walls with white trim, and custard-colored cabinets."

MARK CUTLER

FINE PAINTS OF EUROPE | P11130

"It's an incredibly complex color, a weird combination of yellow and green with this red undertone. Beautiful."

THOMAS JAYNE
BENJAMIN MOORE | SCARECROW 1041

PHILIP GORRIVAN
BENJAMIN MOORE | RAZZLE DAZZLE 1348

"Pick one wall. Apply two coats of Rust-Oleum Magnetic primer, paint it this yummy raspberry color, and then put up your children's artwork, school schedules, and birthday invites with magnets."

....

BARCLAY BUTERA
RALPH LAUREN PAINT | CREAM STONE UL54 (TOP)
| WEATHERED BROWN UL44 (BOTTOM)

"Paint your cabinets Cream Stone, a muted off-white, more gray than yellow. Then use rich, taupey Weathered Brown on the walls for contrast. It makes the kitchen a little more masculine, more sophisticated."

Benjamin Moore's Scarecrow gives a new kitchen wing designed by Thomas Jayne and architect Peter Pennoyer a strong visual link to the 18th-century Virginia home it serves. Benjamin Moore White Dove lifts the raftered ceiling, keeping the mood open and airy.

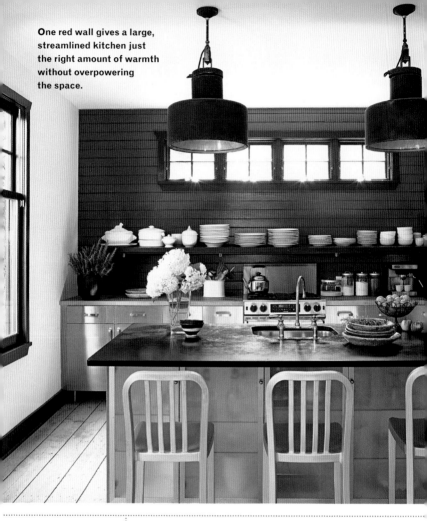

One red wall gives a large, streamlined kitchen just the right amount of warmth without overpowering the space.

AMANDA KEYSER
BENJAMIN MOORE | MERLOT RED 2006-10
A wall painted Merlot sets off white dishware salvaged from a grand seaside hotel in France that was torn down. The kitchen was designed to keep several family cooks from bumping elbows.

ANN MCGUIRE

VALSPAR | SPRING SQUASH 2008-1B

"You're taking a chance with orange, but it can be fabulous. It's playful during the day for kids doing projects, and at night, with the lamps lit, it glows. Start with one wall—that may be enough."

SANDRA NUNNERLEY

BENJAMIN MOORE | WOLF GRAY 2127-40

"I'm so tired of all those off-white cabinets. I'd paint them this dark Swedish gray-blue and make the whole room very Gustavian, with chalky white walls, Carrara marble countertops, and stainless-steel appliances."

JASON BELL

PRATT & LAMBERT | TAMPICO 1411

"In an old kitchen where everything was mismatched shades of white, we needed a distraction. So we painted just the doors, not the frames, of the cabinets this teal green aquamarine and replaced the cheap white plastic knobs with vintage hardware."

MICK DE GIULIO

BENJAMIN MOORE | GREAT BARRINGTON GREEN HC-122

"Especially in a small kitchen, people don't think of dark colors as an option. This is a lovely gray-green, not too dark and very soft, like moss."

WELCOMING BATHROOMS

Whether your style is ready-set-go or long soaks in the tub, these designers will bathe you in just the right color.

Every room deserves one dramatic element, like the oversized mirror hanging over the freestanding tub in this bathroom designed by Michael Smith. To heighten the effect of an old boat window, he placed the mirror against a wall painted a cotton candy blue. The overall effect is a cheery effervescence.

MICHAEL SMITH
PRATT & LAMBERT | COOS BAY 19-31

ANNE CARSON

BENJAMIN MOORE | BRILLIANT WHITE

"In a bathroom, there's nothing better than clean, fresh, pure white. This is a very clear, soothing white, not too bright and not too creamy. You never get tired of it, it never looks dated, and you can easily change the look by changing the artwork."

ATHALIE DERSE

PRATT & LAMBERT | ANTIQUE WHITE 2207

"I want a color that's subtle and refreshing at the same time. This looks like an old celadon that would have been popular back in the 1940s. First thing in the morning, I don't want anything jolting."

....

MICHAEL FORMICA

BENJAMIN MOORE | CALIFORNIA BLUE 2060-20

"It's a strange color, sort of an old-fashioned blue-print blue. I actually like dark bathrooms with very controlled artificial light. I think dark walls are sexy."

....

RONALD BRICKE

PRATT & LAMBERT | AUTUMN CROCUS 1141

"Imagine waking up and walking into the brightest, sunniest day. This is a bright lavender blue, moderately intense, very cheerful. Some people will say, 'Oh, I don't like lavender,' but this is clean, fresh — guaranteed to perk you up."

....

DAVID MANN

RALPH LAUREN PAINT | ARCHITECTURAL CREAM UL 55

"This is kind of a pale khaki gray. It approximates the kind of light you get on a cloudy day, which makes all the other colors around look deep and true, more intense."

CHAD EISNER
PRATT & LAMBERT | SOLITARY 19-29 (TOP)
| SILVER BIRCH 18-31 (BOTTOM)
In this master bathroom, Chad Eisner used a muted olive green to lend weight to the wainscoting and added contrast by painting the walls above a soft sand color. Both colors beautifully complement the elegant sink fixtures and pedestal table.

ROBIN BELL

FARROW & BALL | DIMITY 2008

"This is a beautiful, cloudlike off-white with just the right amount of pink in it, so people look nice—but not so flattering that you walk out the door thinking you look terrific when you really don't."

JARRETT HEDBORG

BENJAMIN MOORE | TANGERINE DREAM 2012-30

"It ain't white, honey. It's a wonderful, glowing Luis Barragán color, an orange that doesn't look silly. The dirty little secret about these big white California Spanish houses is that inside they feel dark and gray. This will make you look 10 years younger."

THAD HAYES

DONALD KAUFMAN COLOR COLLECTION | DKC-64

"It's a dark gray-brown-green, you name it, it's in there. It's almost like a clay mud color—really rich and really beautiful. Very dramatic with dark or light stone and nickel fixtures."

BARBARA SALLICK

BENJAMIN MOORE | SILVER SATIN OC-26

"White is the color of health and hygiene. It has to be the right white, something soft and warm that can complement marble, tile, porcelain, metal."

SUSAN FERRIER
BENJAMIN MOORE | CARRINGTON BEIGE HC-93 (TOP)
SHERWIN-WILLIAMS | BRAINSTORM BRONZE 7033 (BOTTOM)
Susan Ferrier used Carrington Beige, a sort of pebbly taupe, on
the walls of this luxurious master bathroom. A framing effect is
created using Brainstorm Bronze on the French doors looking
out onto a lovely garden.

STEPHANIE STOKES
BENJAMIN MOORE | FRESH DEW 435

"This is in the mint, pine family. It's a pale wash of green that reminds me of the water off Corsica in the summer. Since I spend a lot of time soaking in my Jacuzzi, I can't imagine anything better."

PRISCILLA ULMANN
FARROW & BALL | YELLOW GROUND 218

"This is a rich egg-yolk yellow, a classic English color. I used it in my own bathroom, which doesn't have any windows, and it brings in the sunlight that's not there."

BETSY BROWN
PRATT & LAMBERT | WENDIGO 2293

"This is really, really dark, almost black. It's not a color that introduces anything—you're barely aware of it at all, you just see what's in the room."

RALPH HARVARD
PRATT & LAMBERT | PELHAM GRAY LIGHT CW-819

"It's a very evasive gray from the Colonial Williamsburg line that changes color in different lights. I hate to call it a gray, because people think of gray as chilly, and this is very warm. It can look 1930s chic or 1810 countrified or 21st-century cool."

ELEGANCE IN DINING

The dining room is the ebullient heart of any home. It can be a feast for the eyes—or a convivial backdrop for conversation. Before you set the table, let color set your dining room's mood.

"We chose a dark green for the dining room walls, which is complementary to the red kitchen cabinets. When you have a deep, rich color like that on the walls, with crisp white moldings, you don't need elaborate window treatments."

EMILY O'KEEFE
RALPH LAUREN PAINT | MASTER ROOM VM99

The dining room of this 1920s New England clapboard house is incredibly cozy. The creamy butterscotch paint Jason Bell chose for the walls adds a quietly uplifting element to the room. It softens the sunlight coming through the window.

JASON BELL

BENJAMIN MOORE | HEPPLEWHITE IVORY HC-36

CHARLOTTE MOSS

FARROW & BALL | BREAKFAST ROOM GREEN 81

"When you're eating, you want a space that feels fresh, and green reads fresh to me. This is a crisp celadon. With white linens on a wooden table, it reminds me of eating outdoors. I adore eating outdoors. Everything tastes better—even my cooking!"

ARTHUR DUNNAM

BENJAMIN MOORE | BRANCHPORT BROWN HC-72

"It's a very dark chocolate brown with a bit of red in it, so there's a warm aspect to it that makes people look good. In high gloss, it really sparkles with candlelight. I think chocolate brown particularly suits a city dining room."

CELERIE KEMBLE

FARROW & BALL | MERE GREEN 219

"This is the missing jewel tone we get only in peacock feathers. It's rich and still playful—it can be a formal or sort of decadent color, and it looks beautiful with accents of white lacquer or dark wood."

JEFFREY BILHUBER

BENJAMIN MOORE | WISPY GREEN 414

"A pale, yellow-based spring green is dazzling to the complexion. Greens bring out the pink. Just think what haricots verts do for a lamb chop. It's the perfect foil."

BARCLAY BUTERA

RALPH LAUREN PAINT | CALYPSO VM138

"It's a blue with a certain nobility, something you would have seen in a colonial house in Williamsburg. But it's also a casual and comfortable color. A dining room should be approachable."

MARIETTE HIMES GOMEZ

BENJAMIN MOORE | SAGE TINT 458

"It's kind of robin's egg blue, and with mahogany furniture and neutral upholstery, it looks great. I see dining rooms as mostly evening rooms, and this has life to it. It's very soothing."

The ceiling of the Haines dining room is painted with Farrow & Ball's Babouche 223 (page 155), the moldings with Pointing 2003 (page 24), and the walls with Benjamin Moore's Orange Parrot 2169-20.

MARTYN LAWRENCE-BULLARD
BENJAMIN MOORE | ORANGE PARROT 2169-20
"It's very close to a color in a 1940s Billy Haines house I restored in Beverly Hills. I love pairing it with yellow on the ceilings and ivory crown moldings like he did. Doesn't it sound wild? It's a really exotic fun orange that creates drama, yet lets you know the inhabitant is very playful."

TOM SCHEERER

BENJAMIN MOORE | CHOCOLATE CANDY BROWN 2107-10
          (TOP)
          | ATRIUM WHITE INTERIOR ROOM
          (BOTTOM)

This turn-of-the-century dining room serves as a major household thoroughfare, which presented designer Tom Scheerer with a challenge. He decided to use color to create a sense of intimacy, painting the walls a deep chocolate brown. Paired with a cool white ceiling and crisp trim, the combination gives the spacious room a casual warmth.

COLIN COWIE
BENJAMIN MOORE | SHELBURNE BUFF HC-28

"This is a wonderful oatmeal, camel color. The gold hue makes everybody look like they just came back from somewhere fabulous."

MICHAEL BERMAN
RALPH LAUREN PAINT | DESERT BOOT TH35

"Like a blanket of velvet that wraps the walls—it's a really saturated rich brown, very deep, almost aubergine. It has the feeling of the background in an 18th-century portrait."

BRET WITKE
BENJAMIN MOORE | POWDER SAND 2151-70

"There's a paleness to it but also a warmth. It's like a blank canvas, so anyone who sits in front of it, or any food, any color, looks really attractive—amazing, in fact. Everything pops. The dining room is all about the table and the people sitting at it."

T. KELLER DONOVAN
BENJAMIN MOORE | BROWN SUGAR 2112-20

"If you are a chocoholic like me, you just walk in and get hungry. It's a really rich, deep, milk-chocolatey color, and we did white brackets with white vases all over the walls."

SOFT BEDROOMS

It's the room we see first thing in the morning and last thing at night. We want the colors in our bedroom to be restful and restorative, tranquil and cheerful. And with these colors, that's exactly how you feel.

"You know how some people are not comfortable with silence — they have to fill it up with words? The same can be said for a house. Some people think it has to be filled with stuff to be beautiful. It doesn't. I used color only to set a mood, not as a statement. I like to keep the background simple."

KAY DOUGLASS
BENJAMIN MOORE | SEAPEARL OC-19

WALDO FERNANDEZ
BENJAMIN MOORE | HOLIDAY WREATH 447
This color reminds designer Waldo Fernandez of the color
of wet stone, a cool kind of gray-green, like slate after a
summer rain. It provides an effective backdrop for a series
of framed nature studies that he arranged on the walls of
his son's bedroom.

MARIO BUATTA

BENJAMIN MOORE | MISTY LILAC 2071-70

"What you want is anything that makes a woman look more beautiful. Lavender is great for blondes or brunettes and very pretty with blue-and-white fabric. Just don't tell your husband it's lavender."

T. KELLER DONOVAN

FARROW & BALL | BORROWED LIGHT 235

"The name says it all. It's the palest blue that they make, and it just shimmers. When you walk into a room with white woodwork and this pale blue, you think you're in heaven. My painter went home and told his wife about it, so you know you've got a winner."

ALESSANDRA BRANCA

PRATT & LAMBERT | AVOINE DE MER 17-26

"It's green, somewhere between apple and moss, and it's like waking up in spring every morning."

BIRCH COFFEY

BENJAMIN MOORE | PALE MOON OC-108

"Nothing is more of a turn-on than Champagne, and this is that same uplifting kind of inviting color. In the evening, it looks very warm and rich, and in the morning, there's a happy mood about it."

SUZANNE RHEINSTEIN

RALPH LAUREN PAINT | CRESTED BUTTE NA40

"It's the color of stones under water—relatively dark, but very warm and nuanced. It's wonderful to have a dark bedroom. Aren't there a few people who like to use this room for sleeping?"

SHEILA BRIDGES

FARROW & BALL | GREEN BLUE 84

"It's my two favorite colors mixed together. Soft, but with a lot of vibrancy. Greens and blues are known for their relaxing effect."

BRIAN MCCARTHY

BENJAMIN MOORE | CAYMAN BLUE 2060-50

"I happen to love this color. I've mixed it with black-and-white photography and some pretty serious Empire furniture, and it's really fabulous."

CHARLOTTE MOSS

BENJAMIN MOORE | BLANCHED CORAL 886

"It's a pale, pale, pale, almost fleshy pink, but on the pink side rather than the beige side. It's feminine and soft. It's almost like you've got a little glow in your cheeks. That's what you want in the morning when you wake up and have no makeup on. Green was not going to work for me."

MARSHALL WATSON

DONALD KAUFMAN COLOR COLLECTION | DKC-37

"What I like about Donald Kaufman paints is that they're indescribable. This particular shade has green and blue in it, and brown and gray. A February sea blue. I always use it in flat, so it has this rich velvety quality, like soft moonlight."

DD ALLEN

C2 | BELLA DONNA C2-316 W

"It's a smoky, purply mauve, the color of the sky at sunset. It's a soothing, relaxing, moody color that looks beautiful with raspberry curtains, mauve bedding, and gray flannel carpet."

KATHRYN M. IRELAND

FARROW & BALL | CITRON 74

"It reminds me of the sunflowers that surround my house in France. It's bright, cheerful. Even when it's dark, it's always going to be happy."

MILES REDD

BENJAMIN MOORE | BIRD'S EGG 2051-60

"My bedroom is painted a very pale blue, with touches of silver gray and coral. I'm a Pisces, and I'm always totally gravitating to water and cool colors."

SUZANNE KASLER
GLIDDEN | LIMOGES BLUE 30BG56/045
Suzanne Kasler dreamed up a cool blue bedroom that is the epitome of tranquillity. The black-lacquered bed gives the classic backdrop a contemporary edge.

COLORS
TO BRIGHTEN
YOUR DAY

The shell-splashed fabric on the
armchair and bed is **Concarneau**
from **Pierre Frey.**

COLORS THAT MAKE YOU FEEL GOOD

There's nothing more uplifting than clear yellow, real red, restful blue. Here are twelve shades sure to make you smile.

This blue is cool, restful—there's a sense of depressuring. This guest room reflects a Paula Perlini truism: "Everyone loves blue and white."

PAULA PERLINI
BENJAMIN MOORE | RIVIERA AZURE 822

OPPOSITE PAGE :

"It's a funny combination of pink and red and coral. Colors in that range are very stimulating—good for conversation; they keep people's minds going. It looks luscious in a satin finish."

LIBBY CAMERON

BENJAMIN MOORE | MILANO RED 1313

ROBERT STILIN

FARROW & BALL | COOKING APPLE GREEN 32

"I'm in my office looking out at this field where horses graze, and the sun has turned the grass this rich, vibrant yellowy green, and it just looks so happy."

MARY DOUGLAS DRYSDALE

BENJAMIN MOORE | JAMAICAN AQUA 2048-60

"This is a pale teal, a really lovely neoclassical color that goes with high heels and beautiful earrings and sixteen sets of china."

JOHN YUNIS

FINE PAINTS OF EUROPE | SUNNYSIDE LANE 7014T

"It's hard to get yellow right—usually it's too green or too red or too muddy. But this is nice and clear, without being shrill. If it's too vivid, it's like living in an omelet."

In this living room, Libby Cameron uses white to cool down the red. The chair is painted in $1/2$ **Bright White** and $1/2$ **Linen White**, both by Benjamin Moore.

JAMIE DRAKE

BENJAMIN MOORE | WHITE SATIN 2067-70

"It's an *ahhhhhhhh* color, a pale, ethereal blue with a touch of periwinkle. Completely uplifting—like floating on a cloud surrounded by fluffy down pillows. As soon as you walk in, you feel the weight of the world is lifted from your shoulders."

DAVID MITCHELL
BENJAMIN MOORE | SWEET DREAMS 847

"Sweet Dreams is like a hug. I know that sounds sappy, but this is the perfect nice, comfortable blue, with just enough gray, and just enough robin's egg, and just enough teal. Paint any room with this, and it becomes the happiest room in your house—but not in a clownish, perky way. My kind of happiness means serenity and atmosphere."

SARA BENGUR
DONALD KAUFMAN COLOR COLLECTION | DKC-30

"It's the color of afternoon light—that end-of-the-day moment when it feels warm and mellow and everything has a glow. I'm thinking some beautiful house on the Mediterranean, and we're sitting outside and eating figs with a bottle of white wine."

MATTHEW PATRICK SMYTH

PRATT & LAMBERT | VINTAGE CLARET 1013

"This is a real red, a true red that's not trying to be anything else but red. I used it in my living room, and it never fails to get a reaction. I once had someone look at the color and say, 'I wish I could go through life with these walls behind me.'"

SUSAN ZISES GREEN

DURON MOUNT VERNON ESTATE OF COLOURS
| LEAMON SIRRUP DMV070

"This is the color of a pistachio nut—a clear, sharp yellow-green with no sadness in it at all. I used it in a show house for Kips Bay, and there wasn't a person who came in who did not smile."

THOMAS GUNKELMAN

BENJAMIN MOORE | BLEEKER BEIGE HC-80

"This isn't beige the way we think of beige—so boring. This has warmth and depth. It's a very sophisticated color that makes me feel good and I know I look good against it."

In this dining alcove by Peter Vaughn, the high-gloss floor—painted Benjamin Moore's Mauve Bauhaus 1407—is a darker version of the lavender walls.

PETER VAUGHN
BENJAMIN MOORE | SPRING IRIS 1402
"I started out as a painter, and I'd always add purple to other colors to give them depth and richness. Lavender reflects light well, which is why you see it all over Scandinavia. In the depth of winter, it's a very cheerful color to walk into."

Am
the
at t
cas
colo

ADVENTUROUS REDS

Subtlety is not red's calling card. There are plenty of other colors for that. We look to this life force to be rich and vital—assertive enough to add some needed spark to a scene without screaming.

"We painted the front hall stairwell the color of old Chinese lacquer. We painted it with old-fashioned enamel, too, the kind that takes three days to dry, and then I picked up that color throughout the house."

AMANDA KYSER
BENJAMIN MOORE | MERLOT RED 2006-10

ALISON SPEAR

BENJAMIN MOORE | RUBY RED 2001-10

"Red is a neutral for me. Like red nail polish, it's classic. It goes with everything. I actually had that Coco Chanel red lacquer nail polish matched, and I painted the floors of my living and dining rooms with it. They're the most fun floors I've ever had."

ELDON WONG

BENJAMIN MOORE | REDSTONE 2009-10

Small dose, big impact: Eldon Wong used a rich saturated red on the back interior of the cupboard built into the dining room wall of this 18th-century stone house. The brilliant color perfectly accents a 1950s Rosenthal china service by Raymond Loewy.

RUTHIE SOMMERS

FINE PAINTS OF EUROPE | DUTCHLAC BRILLIANT
TULIP RED W1001B-M

"I prefer the warm, vibrant reds to the historic reds, which are beautiful but sedate. This is a daring red, a real fire engine red. It has a playfulness that reminds me of a little red schoolhouse."

SUZANNE KASLER

RALPH LAUREN PAINT | DRESSAGE RED TH41

"When I look for red, I want a pure, true red, like the color in the American flag. Ralph Lauren does absolutely the best. It's the essence of red. It makes me think of boating or polo."

DAVID EASTON

FARROW & BALL | BLAZER 212

"It's exciting and it has a historical reference: the Greek vases, the palace at Knossos, and all that business. I love red, always have, always will. Either you like steak or you like hamburgers."

MARIO BUATTA

BENJAMIN MOORE | MERLOT RED 2006-10

"I like a touch of red in every room—it brings life, like red lips on a woman. I did an entire library in Merlot. It looked great."

"All my life I've pursued the perfect red. I can never get painters to mix it for me. It's exactly as if I'd said "I want Rococo with a spot of Gothic in it and a bit of Buddhist temple"—they have no idea what I'm talking about."

DIANA VREELAND
BENJAMIN MOORE RED 2000-10

PETER DUNHAM

PRATT & LAMBERT | PAGODA RED 5-15

"It's not too orange, not too blue—it looks like an antique red, a Pompeian red. I used it in a bathroom with white Carrara marble floors from a monastery. It made them sing. Almost everything looks good with it."

JOE NYE

PORTOLA PAINTS | PAPRIKA 013

"This paint has a strié effect, very obvious brush marks that appear as it dries. It can take a drab space and give it dignity. Paprika is warm, welcoming, and slightly dramatic—it makes food look great, people look great, candlelight look great."

There's no red room as famous as Diana Vreeland's "garden in
hell" by Billy Baldwin. The Bracquenié chintz, Le Grand Arbre,
is available to the trade from Pierre Frey. Nobody knows
exactly what red her room was, but we found a good match in
Benjamin Moore Red.

SUZANNE KASLER
GLIDDEN | CHECKERBERRY 32RR50/260
"It's daring, but everyone loves it—a rich peony pink that doesn't look at all little girl–ish. The pink accentuates this smaller area and makes it very cozy. It is important, though, when you use a bold color like this, that you make sure it has enough depth in it. Colors that have no depth are oddly fluorescent. They leap out at you, rather than pull you in."

ELISSA CULLMAN

BENJAMIN MOORE | SANGRIA 2006-20

"Lately I'm on this anti-completely-neutral kick. You have to have some seasoning in your rooms. Sangria is a good, universal-donor red—not too blue, not too orange, not too dark."

RODERICK SHADE

BENJAMIN MOORE | MILLION DOLLAR RED 2003-10

"It's a true, deep red. I like the temperature of it: it's a bit cooler. But a little red goes a long way. It's good in areas where you don't spend much time or in boring areas that need a strong burst of color."

WILLIAM DIAMOND AND ANTHONY BARATTA

RALPH LAUREN PAINT | LATTICE RED IB57

"Red never goes out of style. It's full of life—always fresh, always fun to wake up to. We go for reds with less blue in them and more orange because they're happier to live with."

ALEXA HAMPTON

BENJAMIN MOORE | TUCSON RED 1300

"This is a very bricky red. I prefer the warmth of earth tones to the bluer reds, which are trickier—some make me think of nail polish. I'm fine with bluer reds on my toes, but not necessarily on my walls."

COLOR
FOR COZINESS

You know the kind of rooms we're talking about: warm, intimate, homey. They're decked with comfortable colors; colors that remind you of the soft gray of an old wool blanket.

In this romantic homage to the 1920s Spanish-style Mizner houses, designer Fern Santini painted new kitchen cabinets Nantucket Gray and treated them with a custom sienna glaze.

FERN SANTINI

BENJAMIN MOORE | NANTUCKET GRAY HC-111

MARSHALL WATSON

SHERWIN-WILLIAMS | HUMBLE GOLD SW6380

"Humble Gold has such warmth on a gray winter day. It just snuggles into you. There are so many colors in it—gold, yellow, pink, red. That little blush brings out the rosiness in your cheeks when you come in from the cold. It's not a sharp color. That's what makes it cozy and inviting."

STEPHANIE STOKES

FARROW & BALL | CLAYDON BLUE 87

"My library gets no light, so I took advantage of the disadvantage and painted it this deep blue-green. It's a restful color, kind of an ancient color. You see it in the medieval tapestries at the Cluny Museum. Now everybody gravitates to my dark, cozy room. And the color works with anything— Oriental rugs, African pillows, Islamic textiles."

TODD ROMANO
FARROW & BALL | BLAZER 212

"**Red is not a color for sissies, but you can't go wrong with this good orangey red that reminds me of carved cinnabar boxes from China. It's warm and cheerful with chintz. Or add a coat of gloss for a lacquered effect and the room will feel like a glamorous jewel box.**"

PATRICIA HILL

DONALD KAUFMAN COLOR COLLECTION | DKC-11

"This is about atmosphere. It's a really soft shade of green—a pale, pale sage. Very soothing. It's a Donald Kaufman color, which means it will be different depending on the light, and that makes it interesting. I like it with a muted paisley or one of those tea-stained English linens made by Robert Kime or Bennison."

MICHAEL WHALEY

BENJAMIN MOORE | GARDEN CUCUMBER 644

"To me, cozy is a dark color like this green, with just a trace of blue. It's the color of the green baize door in an old English country house. Cozy needs to be small, intimate, a place where you can curl up with a drink by the fire. Dark, rich colors actually make me feel introspective. Bring in some deep wood tones and a bit of gilt for some sparkle."

FRANKLIN SALASKY

BENJAMIN MOORE | MUSTANG 2111-30

"In an all-white house, I'll often do one room, like the study or the TV room, that's a total reversal. I'll paint it very dark, like this espresso brown, so you have a completely different feeling. Darkness creates intimacy. Bring in deep blues and reds. Actually, every color looks good with it."

MICHAEL ROBERSON

BENJAMIN MOORE | POWELL BUFF HC-35

"This wonderful warm tan is almost the color of dried wheat. What makes it so pretty is the way it reacts to light. When the sun hits it, it glows, and on a rainy day it casts a nice kind of cozy warm shadow on the room. Very calming in a bedroom. Great in a sitting room with almond-colored suede or gray flannel."

JOHN SALADINO

MARTIN SENOUR | MARKET SQUARE TAVERN

DARK GREEN CW401

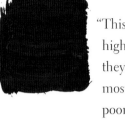

"This is a beautiful deep inky green. Use it in a high-gloss, oil-based paint—first prep the walls so they're absolutely smooth—and it will make the most dismal room feel warm and rich. I call it the poor man's paneling. Great in a library, or an entrance hall where it would make the living room beyond seem bigger, lighter, brighter."

TORI GOLUB

DONALD KAUFMAN COLOR COLLECTION | DKC-62

"At first glance, this is a soft grayish putty. Then its golden undertones unfold as it catches the light and it radiates with warmth. It's like pale ashes with hidden embers glowing beneath them. It's an old warmth, and the color is always changing."

CHRISTOPHER MAYA

FARROW & BALL | RECTORY RED 217

"Red is one of those colors that is inherently cozy. But it's a difficult color to get right. Either it gets very rusty or it becomes too saturated and bright. But this has enough blue in it so it doesn't go into fire-engine mode. It's a refined red. It makes you feel special."

BARBARA WESTBROOK
BENJAMIN MOORE | WHITALL BROWN HC-69 (TOP)
| OVERCAST OC-43 (BOTTOM)
Designer Barbara Westbrook chose a satiny khaki green
for the walls of this paneled study. It's a very serene
color and the off-white on the ceiling provides
a needed contrast. The sunlight adds a natural glow
throughout the room.

MYRA HOEFER

RALPH LAUREN PAINT | CALIFORNIA POPPY GH170

"I saw Andrew Lloyd Webber's music room, and
now I want to paint everything this color. It's a
true tangerine orange, and they must have put a
squirt of burnt umber in the glaze, because it's
like a nicotine stain. It looks old and rich and
warm. The room glows. It's like having a fabulous
pashmina scarf wrapped around you."

Benjamin Moore's Super White, already on the walls of Thomas Jayne's New York loft, turned out to be the perfect backdrop for his vibrant color blocks.

QUICK COLOR FIXES

Is there a dark corner of your dining room that you'd like to brighten up? Or do you want to add a little zest to a room? Here are some easy color tricks to add a bit of design flair.

"When I moved into a big white loft, all my furniture looked lost. So I painted these floating cubes of color on the walls to anchor a few pieces, and it had this great effect. Absolutely transporting."

THOMAS JAYNE
BENJAMIN MOORE | SMASHING PINK 1303 (TOP)
| BLUE BELLE 782 (BOTTOM)

Rather than scrap the 1980s maple bookcases in this California living room, designer Jay Jeffers updated them with paint.

JAY JEFFERS
BENJAMIN MOORE | BUXTON BLUE HC-149 (TOP)
| RUST 2175-30 (BOTTOM)
"It's the contrast of cool Wedgewood blue with terra-cotta that makes this bookcase interesting. If I had painted it all blue, it would have dissapeared. But now the dark paint on the back wall makes a dramatic backdrop for all the family photos and accessories."

CHRISTOPHER COLEMAN

BENJAMIN MOORE | COOL AQUA 2056-40

"Why not put the color in the closet? Nothing like being a little uncomfortable arriving for dinner, the host takes your coat, opens the closet door, and wow! You get a big dose of turquoise. It gets the conversation going—and distracts from the mess."

SUZANNE KASLER

FARROW & BALL | ORANGERY 70

"Paint one wall and it will change the whole feel of a room. I'd use this vibrant, earthy orange in a dining room, on the wall with the buffet, and bring in more color with decorative items."

MILES REDD

BENJAMIN MOORE | ICY BLUE 2057-70 (TOP)

| HERITAGE RED EXTERIOR ROOM (BOTTOM)

"People never think about doors and ceilings as places for color. Think how chic it would be to have chalky white walls with black, black, trim, a pale blue ceiling, and lipstick red doors—in high gloss. Blue and red look so regal. It would make eveyone feel like the Duke of Windsor."

LARRY LASLO

BENJAMIN MOORE | LADYBUG RED 1322

"I love to see a painted staircase—not the tread itself, but the vertical part. Most people leave it white, but it always gets kicked up. So make it barn red—just flat, clear, clean color."

ALESSANDRA BRANCA

DONALD KAUFMAN COLOR COLLECTION | DKC-23

"Update a plain white kitchen with apple green stripes—vertical, definitely. Ten inches wide if the ceiling is eight feet high or less."

TOM STRINGER

RALPH LAUREN PAINT | PRUSSIAN BLUE VM122

"Paint the interior of the lampshades. Then you have these white card stock shades with a little peek of color—like this beautiful, watercolory Easter egg shade of blue."

BIRCH COFFEY

BENJAMIN MOORE | CARBON COPY 2117-10

"I stole this from a friend born in Baltimore, where at some point it became very fashionable to paint your baseboards black. Just the flat part, not the upper molding. Instantly you get this crisp graphic element, as if you've underlined the room."

**BENJAMIN MOORE
SUMMER BLUE 2067-50**
A well-placed jolt of color
can have a surprising
impact on a room. Choose
this richly saturated blue to
set off the softer blues in
the ceiling wallpaper.

WHITNEY STEWART

C2 | CAFÉ LATTE 7314 (TOP)

| CHAI 7293 (BOTTOM)

"Make your own virtual moldings. Do circles within
squares or simple rectangles. I like this warm,
pretty brown against a straw color. Get out an
inch-wide brush and just start painting. If it's all
perfectly taped out, it loses its charm."

Sometimes the best place for color isn't on the wall. Color consultant Eve Ashcraft used a muted peridot paint on the floorboards, injecting a splash of gemlike color into an all-white bathroom. Using durable oil gloss enamel ensures a hard-wearing finish.

GIL SCHAFER AND EVE ASHCRAFT
PRATT & LAMBERT | PERIDOT 18-20

DD ALLEN
MODERN MASTERS | VENETIAN BLUE ME-429

"Don't forget the floor—it's such an underutilized opportunity for color. In a downtown loft, we were going for a Moroccan feeling, with limed white walls and a Mediterranean blue floor for a wonderful cool, watery feeling. It's a metallic paint, so it really sparkles."

KELLY WEARSTLER
PRATT & LAMBERT | SCARLET O'HARA 1870

"Color on the ceiling is very tempting, like dipping your toe in the pool. I would use a really beautiful red. Some are too purple but this has more orange, which I think is a little sexier. It definately makes a space feel more intimate and gives some energy."

In a very theatrical decision, the chair was lacquered to a high sheen using **Aqua Pigmented Gloss Black Lacquer** and covered in white vinyl.

ACCENTS ON FURNITURE

Give an old chair, bureau, or dresser that attitude adjustment. White places the emphasis on form, while daring color will play up an otherwise overlooked personality that can give your whole room a lift.

Small elements add drama to a room. Woodson and Rummerfield painted the foyer wall a serene sage green to highlight the lovely off-white Sunset mirror and an Asian-inspired console. For an extra touch of glamour, a vintage parlor chair was added.

RON WOODSON AND JAIME RUMMERFIELD
SHERWIN-WILLIAMS | HAZEL 6471

CARLETON VARNEY

BENJAMIN MOORE | SUPER WHITE INTERIOR ROOM (TOP)
| LITTLE ANGEL 318 (BOTTOM)

"Dorothy Draper had no qualms about painting a 17th-century chair white—always a white white, never a creamy white. Her attitude was: I'll make antiques work for me. I'd paint a big armoire white, with yellow trim, and display blue-and-white porcelain against the yellow inside."

BRUCE BIERMAN

PRATT & LAMBERT | AUTUMN CROCUS 1141

"This is a soft, muted lavender with a bit of blue in it. I'd put it on a reproduction Louis XVI chair, in high gloss, because that's what makes it modern, and I'd find a fabric for it in exactly the same shade—shiny, like a cotton chintz or vinyl."

CAREY MALONEY

DONALD KAUFMAN COLOR COLLECTION | DKC-10

"I have a big, hugely functional Georgian Revival lawyer's desk in tired dry mahogany, bought from a tired dry lawyer. I painted it this pale gray-green in an oil-base satin finish, cleanable, very calm, but not so pale that it dies. The gimmick is the old-fashioned desk in an unexpected color. It catches light and makes for a more interesting surface."

RUTHIE SOMMERS
RALPH LAUREN PAINT
RELAY RED IB11

"I found this chair in Florida on the Dixie Highway and fell in love with the high fretwork back. In brown it looked dreary, so I painted it pomegranate red. It turned out so well I'm going to reproduce it."

It's not a real **Chippendale** chair, but who cares when it's painted such a delicious red? **Farrow & Ball's Green Ground 206 on the walls** is the perfect complement.

BRIAN MCCARTHY

OLD FASHIONED MILK PAINT CO. | SLATE (TOP)

| OYSTER WHITE (BOTTOM)

"Find a piece that has good lines and trick it up. I've taken a plain pine chest of drawers from a junk shop and done a simple, cottagey finish with milk paint. Start with a base in Swedish blue-gray and lightly brush over it with white, pulling back with steel wool in spots to reveal more color."

CHRISTOPHER MAYA
PRATT & LAMBERT | BLUEBERRY MYRTILLE 1208-3
"I designed that secretary a few years ago for myself, and now it's part of our furniture line. We lacquered it in Heritage Red to add a bit of drama. I just thought red would be the perfect color against that blue. The blue becomes bluer when you see red against it; the red becomes redder."

WILLIAM DIAMOND

BENJAMIN MOORE | ESSEX GREEN EXTERIOR ROOM

"Unless you have beautiful antique wicker with the original stain, you have to paint it, and Essex Green just looks right. It's rich and dark, as dark as you can go and still come off as green, and it works with any fabric. It's instant class, elegant, uncontrived."

KIM ALEXANDRIUK

FARROW & BALL | BABOUCHE 223

"In a guest room that seems a little staid, paint the bed. This is a Ming yellow like you see in Chinese silk robes, with a little lemon and mustard in it, which gives it more dimension."

THOMAS BURAK

BENJAMIN MOORE | HERITAGE RED EXTERIOR ROOM

"Take one of those dated five- or six-arm metal chandeliers that you can find at flea markets or on eBay, and paint it lipstick red in a high-gloss finish. Top it off with cream-colored shades, and it will glam up any room."

OPPOSITE PAGE :

"On this vintage dresser, which makes a great nightstand, we accented the handles and the box with Swiss Coffee and painted the drawers Winter White. We used flat paint with three coats of semigloss clear coat on top—that way you can really control the sheen."

ROBERT WILLSON

BENJAMIN MOORE | SWISS COFFEE OC-45 (TOP)

| WINTER WHITE 2140-70 (BOTTOM)

MARIO BUATTA

BENJAMIN MOORE | WINDHAM CREAM HC-6

"I'm always having old dining room chairs stripped and painted—so light and airy, rather than the heavy thud of old brown wood. Or just buy new ones at the Door Store and paint them this lovely pale yellow, like the inside of a banana."

MOLLY LUETKEMEYER

DUNN-EDWARDS | AFTER THE STORM DE5769

"One of those inexpensive, gaudy mirrors with a lot of carving can actually become quite beautiful with paint. I like this deep, muted teal because it's mysterious. You can't quite figure out if it's blue or green. Colors like this with a little gray in them take you to the next level of sophistication."

The two-tone effect shows off the details on a Greek Key chest made by Kittinger back in the 1940s.

KATIE RIDDER

FARROW & BALL | BLAZER 212

"I'd paint the base of a sofa, if it's a framed sofa with maybe just a strip of wood along the bottom and tapered feet. Paint all the wood this pretty, fresh Chinese red. It's an easy thing to do, and that little detail will really make it snap."

In the 1960s, David Hicks designed his Chelsea apartment and lacquered the walls of his living room in a color he called "Coca-Cola."

COLOR WE'VE BEEN DYING TO TRY

What colors do designers really, *really* want to use, but haven't had the chance yet? They're just waiting for the right room.

"This room, lacquered a "Coca-Cola" color, sealed it—David Hicks was the James Bond of interior design. Wow! It's a great bold sexy statement. I would do it in this very dark brown, in a full gloss finish as he did, so it becomes luminous."

PETER DUNHAM
FARROW & BALL | MAHOGANY 36

BOBBY MCALPINE

RALPH LAUREN PAINT | WALTON CREAM VM65 (TOP)
| LINEN UL03 (BOTTOM)

"I'm aching to do pink. This particular shade is sort of an apparition, like something that used to be pink and this is all that's left of it. Very, very tender. I'd pair it with a nice stone color that would kindly allow the pink to step one little foot forward. For the fabrics, just change the texture — cashmere, powdery silk, nubby wool. Be enveloped by it."

STEPHEN SHUBEL

KELLY-MOORE | CACTUS CAFÉ KM3431-3

"There's a café in Paris that has this unusual green on the walls, a kind of old-world color that makes you feel relaxed and calm. Think of a mossy garden after the rain."

BRETT BELDOCK

BENJAMIN MOORE | GRAPPA 1393

"My dear departed Ron Grimaldi was the most elegant man, totally over the top, and he painted everything eggplant. It looked deep and mysterious and kind of sexy. I see it with silver, light blue, green, orange. I'd treat it as a neutral so I wouldn't be afraid of it."

MARY McDONALD
BENJAMIN MOORE | CORAL PINK 2003-50

"I have a huge drawer for any color I come across that I like. Right now it contains a pink napkin from the Beverly Hills Hotel, a shard from a broken green vase, tear sheets from magazines, some chocolate-covered coffee beans, and red and soft pink boxes from a Paris pastry shop. I had to buy pastries in order to get the boxes."

MARY DOUGLAS DRYSDALE

BEHR | YAM 290B-7

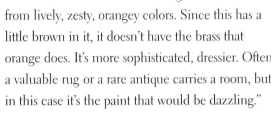

"I love the warmth and inferred light that comes from lively, zesty, orangey colors. Since this has a little brown in it, it doesn't have the brass that orange does. It's more sophisticated, dressier. Often a valuable rug or a rare antique carries a room, but in this case it's the paint that would be dazzling."

DAN BARSANTI

BENJAMIN MOORE | ALLIGATOR ALLEY 441

"In *The War of the Roses*, Danny DeVito's office was the hottest-looking thing I've ever seen. Every nook and cranny was painted this great loden green, with a bit of yellow in it, which makes it look more hip than hunter green. It's a classic luxe look—a great backdrop for books, art, mahogany furniture."

RODERICK SHADE

BENJAMIN MOORE | PINK CORSAGE 1349

"I bought a vintage *Superfly* movie poster in this fuschia. Then I saw kind of '60s cut velvet by Osborne & Little in fuchsia and taupe and thought this was the start of a color scheme. Fuchsia is rockin'. I like the way it pairs with strong neutrals like taupe and wenge brown."

ANGIE HRANOWSKY
BENJAMIN MOORE
WHITE CHOCOLATE OC-127
"Don't get me wrong, I love
white, but I love it for contrast. I see an all-white room
and I think oh, man, that's
great, but if you'd throw some
fuchsia pillows on that
sofa . . . I kept this bedroom
mostly neutral, adding pops
of color for a romantic,
feminine quality."

WHITNEY STEWART

C2 | ENOKI 425

"I'm always looking for the new neutral. This is it,
a soft camel that has red and green and yellow in
it. That's why it goes with everything. Can't you
just imagine it with icy blues? Chutney orange
and sage? Or black and white—always smart.
When a color transcends itself to coordinate with
so many different colors and still retains warmth,
it jumps to that ethereal level. It's a color you just
love to be around. You would feel like a million
dollars in a room painted this color."

MARK EPSTEIN

BENJAMIN MOORE | DEEP RIVER 1582

"Paint a room this warm charcoal gray, with dove white trim, and you'd get an instant sense of architecture. It has all the warmth and coziness of a paneled room and the fantastic, moody, earthy stonelike walls convey a sense of drama."

FRANK ROOP

C2 | EXPEDITION 162

"An intense olive brown with undernotes of chartreuse. It would look amazing in matte on the walls and high gloss on the ceiling."

....

ERINN VALENCICH

DUNN-EDWARDS | DEEP CARNATION DE5011

"David Weidman did these really cool color-block prints in the '70s. The one I have is reds layered with purples and this intense deep violet pink. I see it with a funky mustardy green or turquoise."

....

RICHARD MISHAAN

BENJAMIN MOORE | CHILI PEPPER 2004-20

"This is a really deep coral, kind of like a cheerful Chinese red. Pinks and reds to me are synonymous with frozen drinks and relaxing."

OPPOSITE PAGE :

The buttery yellow on the walls of this preteen boy's room contrasts sharply with the white ribs of the over-hang, creating the effect of a ship's berth.

JODI MACKLIN

DONALD KAUFMAN COLOR COLLECTION | DKC-20

Dark brown plays up the gleaming lines
of modern furniture. And bright green
leaves pop.

COLORS **MEN LOVE**

He may be bold at work and at play, but when it comes to picking colors for his home, he plays it safe. Here are some colors that will encourage a guy to take some chances.

"This dark, warm, rich bronze is very, very sexy. Strong and masculine, yet it doesn't shout. It can take any room from casual to sophisticated. It works really well with metal furniture. I've put purple and lavender, yellow and orange up against it, and they really set each other off."

PHILIP NIMMO
BENJAMIN MOORE | NORTH CREEK BROWN 1001

MARY McDONALD
RALPH LAUREN | YELLOWHAMMER GH100
"Men are open to a soft yellow. When their wives are trying
to do something too pastelly, they'll say, "How about
yellow? I can deal with yellow." It's classic, neutral, safe.
I can't tell you how many yellow living rooms I've done.
This is a wonderful butter yellow, a little dirty, which takes
the girly part out of it."

MARTYN LAWRENCE-BULLARD
FARROW & BALL | RADICCHIO 96

"My current favorite, I confess, is burgundy. For years it was considered outmoded, but now it looks fresh again. Try lacquering the walls of a study in Farrow & Ball's classic burgundy, and contrast it with ivory-painted bookcases and creamy glove-leather club chairs. So chic. Throw in a Paul Evans table or two and you just became the hippest man-about-town."

MARIO BUATTA
BENJAMIN MOORE | GREAT BARRINGTON GREEN HC-122

"Most men are clueless about color. If I ask a man, 'What color is your bedroom?' he says, 'I have to ask my wife.' They stick with safe colors. But they do like this green. It's a yellowy olive green, more contemporary than dark hunter green. I see it in a library with white woodwork."

JAMIE DRAKE
BENJAMIN MOORE | ARUBA BLUE 2048-30

"We painted a library a vibrant shade of turquoisey green—a modern twist on a classic tradition. And then we did all the woodwork in high-gloss black. Very chic, yet totally masculine—like a two-tone Bugatti from the 1920s."

THOMAS JAYNE

BENJAMIN MOORE | CAMEL BACK 1103

"It's just an extremely flattering color, and camel-colored walls are warm and soft, yet very masculine. Camel, with an underpinning of yellow and a slight bit of red, has much more life than beige, which can go gray and cold. Art looks great on it."

MILES REDD

FINE PAINTS OF EUROPE | COLONIAL ROSE 7102T

"I had a client, a very elegant man in his seventies, who requested a pink bedroom. He was a widower, and it reminded him of his wife. I think men like pink more than they're willing to admit. Men tend to like warm colors. This pink has a happy carnation quality in bright sunlight and gets more glowy and dusty at night."

PETER DUNHAM

BENJAMIN MOORE | CITRUS BLAST 2018-30 (TOP)
| MYSTICAL GRAPE 2071-30 (BOTTOM)

"If you're trying to sell a guy on color, just pick the colors of his favorite sports team. The Lakers' colors are the choice of every man in L.A. I have even done the felt on a pool table. I think I should do a line of fabrics—stripes—based on the colors of famous teams."

PAULA PERLINI

BENJAMIN MOORE | MOROCCAN RED 1309

In this library designed by Paula Perlini, the high wainscot, painted a cool white, is a crisp conterpart to the eye-catching strip of red.

The soft chai color designer Stephen Brady chose for this bedroom lends a depth and Old World sophistication to the walls. The warmth and matte velvet texture of the paint anchor the overall palette and serves to beautifully highlight the British Colonial feel of the furnishings.

STEPHEN BRADY
SHERWIN-WILLIAMS | BAGEL 6114

PHOEBE HOWARD
BENJAMIN MOORE | SOFT PUMPKIN 2166-40

"I was doing a high-rise beach condo in Florida in greens and blues and sandy colors, and the husband kept trying to throw in some orange. I said, 'No, no, no. I'm only using colors you can see around here.' So he invited me over for cocktails one night and took me to the window when the sun was setting. 'See? What about that?'"

CLODAGH
BENJAMIN MOORE | MIDNIGHT NAVY 2067-10

"Ask any man what his favorite color is, and he'll probably say blue. It's a thoughtful color. There's a mystery to deep, deep indigo blue. Beautiful in a bedroom—it helps promote sleep. I love it with golds and burnished metallics. It's limitless."

KEITH IRVINE

BENJAMIN MOORE | CORAL GABLES 2010-40

"I've done a lot of rooms for men in paneled wood
and leather. Then I'll highlight the back of a
bookcase with a bit of lively coral. Men like that
color because it reminds them of something to
drink. Add an animal print—Stark's Ocelot
carpet. Supermasculine and comfortable."

CHAPTER 3

INSPIRATION FROM AROUND THE WORLD

Black and white and green is eye-catching, and in this study
Minster Green becomes a strong, unexpected backdrop to a collection
of photography.

COLOR FROM
YOUR TRAVELS

Visiting a new place gives us unfor-
gettable influences: the fiery red
of a Masai *shúkà*; Greece's brilliant
cerulean blue island rooftops; the
dark smoky taupe of the Caspian Sea.

"I was on safari in South Africa at the
Royal Malewane, the most extraordinary private game reserve. When a
dazzle of zebras ran in front of our
jeep, it took my breath away to see
those stripes framed against the bush."

MARTYN LAWRENCE-BULLARD
FARROW & BALL | MINSTER GREEN 224

JEFFREY BILHUBER

FINE PAINTS OF EUROPE | 2030-G70Y

"I've been spending more time in Santa Barbara, up in the hills where you see a particular yellow-based green. It's kind of a cross-pollination of sage and olive and eucalyptus and palm. Not a grass green but a salty green, as if it has a hint of the ocean."

"**The hint of lilac in my mother's Oushak rug inspired the wall color in the living room. Then I pulled fuchsia, raspberry, and orange accents from the painting on the mantel and mixed them with golden yellow. The colors absolutely sing in that room.**"

ANGIE HRANOWSKY
PORTER PAINTS | PERSIAN PINK 6650-1

SUZANNE RHEINSTEIN
RALPH LAUREN PAINT | BLUE-GREEN GH81

"Lago Argentino is a glacier lake in Patagonia, and it's the most amazing color, an aqua, milky because as the ice melts it pulls minerals off the mountain. I stayed in an inn with a stunning view of the Perito Moreno glacier."

PETER DUNHAM
BENJAMIN MOORE | BLUE ANGEL 2058-70

"I was in Oranienbaum in Russia, wandering through this tumbledown park, and suddenly there was this pavilion that looked like a delicately iced wedding cake, painted the blue of a Baltic summer sky. So romantic, and it turns out to have been the takeoff point for an 18th-century royal roller coaster."

ELISSA CULLMAN
BENJAMIN MOORE | DALILA 319

"One of my favorite spots in Florence is sitting on the balcony of the Lungarno Hotel—all those shades of sun drenched yellow. It's a color you see in every Italian town; you wonder how they got it so right."

....

KATHRYN M. IRELAND
RALPH LAUREN PAINT | GOLDFINCH GH105

"Lecce, Italy, is famous for its Baroque architecture— it's that plaster that looks good only after 400 years. And it changes in different lights—apricot one minute and almost burnt siena the next."

....

SUSAN ZISES GREEN
FARROW & BALL | MENAGERIE 63

"We were driving in the countryside outside of Delhi and saw all these women out in the fields in their exquisite saris, in every shade from yellow to gold to this luscious melony terra-cotta."

....

SARA BENGUR
FARROW & BALL | BLUE GROUND 210

"I always visit the harem at the Topkapi Palace, Istanbul, where the sultan lived with hundreds of women. You see this vivid turquoise on the 16th-century tiles along the walls."

ALEX PAPACHRISTIDIS

BENJAMIN MOORE | OPAL ESSENCE 680

"Ever since I was a teenager, we've been going to the Hotel du Cap on the French Riviera and staying at Eden Roc, right on the water with the waves crashing against the rocks. The Mediterranean is deep aqua and I wanted to re-create that feeling, but in a lighter version for a bedroom's walls—a kind of sea foamy aqua."

Walking through this guest bedroom makes you as if you are wading through the lakes of color consultant Eve Ashcraft's Michigan childhood.

GIL SCHAFER AND EVE ASHCRAFT

PRATT & LAMBERT
  | FRESH CREAM 11-5 (TOP)
  | WINDSOR BLUE 27-19 (BOTTOM)

Raspberry with cream: In this octagonal
anteroom between master bedroom and
bath, Gary McBournie added a dollop of
Benjamin Moore's White Dove on the trim.

SUNNY
SUMMER DAYS

What is the palette of summer? Is it the soft pink of cherry Italian ice or the icy green of crushed mint leaves at the bottom of a mojito? Explore the colors of summer and make them your own.

"I like the warmth and cheeriness of this really deep raspberry, almost the color of a pink Corvette. It has that nice old Florida look, before everyone went beige. You need an intense color down here to absorb the light."

GARY MCBOURNIE
BENJAMIN MOORE | FLORIDA PINK 1320

Aqua and pale blues are always evocative of the ocean. In the upstairs hallway of this Long Island beach house, designer Ruthie Sommers chose a color that feels very much like the color of water in the shallows of the Caribbean. An added decorative element—an apothecary jar filled with seashells—summons up memories of tranquil hours at the beach.

RUTHIE SOMMERS

BENJAMIN MOORE | SEA FOAM 2123-60

CARL D'AQUINO

BENJAMIN MOORE | POTPOURRI GREEN 2029-50

"I'm just back from Milan, where I ate gelato twice a day. Such amazing colors! Pistachio is my favorite, but I don't want to gain weight so I'll just surround myself with this creamy green, instead of eating it."

JARRETT HEDBORG

BENJAMIN MOORE | SANTA MONICA BLUE 776

"This deep indigo blue is a classic beach house color. After three hours of sitting in traffic on an August afternoon, you want to collapse in a room that will complement an ice-cold martini."

TIMOTHY WHEALON

RALPH LAUREN PAINT | BASALT VM121

"It feels like fresh air when you walk into the room. And it does read as blue—the palest, softest blue, as if you were floating in the sky. Very ethereal and dreamy."

MARSHALL WATSON

BENJAMIN MOORE | CHIC LIME 396

"Anything with lime speaks of summer to me. This hot green has a lot of yellow. It combines the heat of the sun with the coolness of a gin and tonic on the veranda."

JACKIE TERRELL

BENJAMIN MOORE | LEMON FREEZE 2025-50

"This is an acidy yellow green, kind of hip and very sunny, but not in a cornball way. More exotic, like a color you'd see on a tropical island."

CELERIE KEMBLE

ROLLINSON HUES | 31

"Christopher Rollinson's paints have such saturation and depth. This warm, luminous green feels as fresh and summer sweet as a box of sugar snap peas and captures the very essence of a farmer's market."

LEE MELAHN
BENJAMIN MOORE | PERSIAN VIOLET 1419

"We pulled this lavender from the evening sky and summer flowers like lilac and lupine. In the bright sun, it takes on a warmth that brings out the red in the purple, but then as the light fades, it cools down and becomes this beautiful blue."

JENNIFER GARRIGUES
PORTER PAINTS | PARSLEY TINT 6998-1
This pale aqua green is like the ocean when it's so clear you can see the sand through the water. It reminds me of holidays and sunshine and how calm you feel when you sit on the shore and watch the waves breaking.

In this Florida bedroom by Jennifer Garrigues, sea green walls are set off by a Benjamin Moore white on the trim.

MYRA HOEFER

BENJAMIN MOORE | QUEEN ANNE PINK HC-60

The pink walls of this bedroom remind designer Myra Hoefer of a worn and beloved pair of ballet slippers: silky, soft, and subtle. The color brings this antique red lacquer desk to life.

FRANK ROOP

BENJAMIN MOORE | SOFT FERN 2144-40

"For me, the most appealing colors in summer are not hot but cool. You don't need to be reminded of the sun and heat—you're in it. What you want is a cool breeze through the pine trees, like this chalky gray green."

MIMI MCMAKIN

SHERWIN-WILLIAMS | IN THE PINK SW 6583

"Here in Florida, I have the most wonderful porch that has been painted pink for 30 years. It's the pink of strawberry ice cream cones and climbing roses and the blush on our cheeks after a long, luxurious day at the beach."

MAUREEN FOOTER

BENJAMIN MOORE | OLD WORLD 2011-40

"Imagine walking right into a peony. This color is on the cusp between pink and coral, with a yellow undertone that makes it more sophisticated and versatile than a pinky pink. If only it could smell like a flower!"

The ottoman is covered in Mayfair stripe in plum by Randolph & Hein. The cast-resin floor lamp is by Oly Studio.

FOR A
SUNNY ROOM

Should you go bright to stand up to the sun or soft and cool to subdue it? Designers share their brilliant strategies for using color to capture and tame sunlight.

"This is an elegant yacht, and here is a beautiful custom 1930s-style bed upholstered in white piqué and nailhead trim, looking out of a large porthole. And the view, oh my gosh! This is not your classic blue and white room. It's sweet and understated."

MYRA HOEFER
BENJAMIN MOORE | MISTY MEMORIES 2118-60

EUGENIE NIVEN

BENJAMIN MOORE | SEAFOAM GREEN 2039-60

"It's a cool, minty green, like those striped cabañas on the beach in St. Tropez in the 1940s. I would never paint a really sunny room yellow. You'd feel like you were sitting on the surface of the sun."

JACKYE LANHAM

SHERWIN-WILLIAMS | MAGNETIC GRAY SW-7058

"In the South, sunny means hot. We don't want colors that make you turn the air-conditioning up. This is a silvery blue-gray, almost like an Armani color, very soothing. Because of the grayness, it absorbs light."

DIANE CHAPMAN

BENJAMIN MOORE | TANGERINE FUSION 083

"Something like chrome yellow or shocking pink would be too intense. But this color is just divine. It reminds me of walking into a frothy orangeade or floating on a scoop of orange sherbet."

DAN CARITHERS

BENJAMIN MOORE | FERNWOOD GREEN 2145-40

"This is a green that has a slight haze to it, like early-morning dew on a lawn. You know it's green, but it doesn't reek of it. At different times of the day, it changes color, but it's always still with you."

RUBY BEETS
BENJAMIN MOORE | SMOKE EMBERS 1466
This subtle gray chosen by designer Ruby Beets provides a quiet contrast to the stark white of the ceiling and trim. It also uses the sunlight to elegantly highlight the texture of the plank walls in the living room.

In Nancy Braithwaite's Atlanta bedroom, moldings and baseboards in Pratt & Lambert's Pearly Gates 2268 provide a graphic contrast to dark walls.

NANCY BRAITHWAITE
BENJAMIN MOORE | VAN BUREN BROWN HC-70
"When you go out into the sun, the first thing you do is put on sunglasses. You want to tamp down the glare, so your eyes don't squint. This is a deep tobacco brown that will give a room a certain sense of depth and character, even if it has absolutely no architectural interest."

JOSIE MCCARTHY
SHERWIN-WILLIAMS | IVOIRE SW6127

"This is a scrumptious color that reminds me of my favorite patisserie in Paris, where they have this wonderful yellow cake with raspberry sauce."

....

MARTYN LAWRENCE-BULLARD
FARROW & BALL | BLUE GROUND 210

"There is nothing more uplifting than a room not only drenched in sunshine but also in color. I love the way this turquoise makes me feel, especially when the sun hits it."

....

MICHAEL BERMAN
DUNN-EDWARDS | PERFECT PEAR DE5519

"It's an absolutely amazing color—pear green with a bit of apple. It goes from being pale in the early morning to something that's bright and pungent in the late afternoon."

....

JACKIE TERRELL
PRATT & LAMBERT | NASTURTIUM 1830 (TOP)
| GLOAMING 2145 (BOTTOM)

"If I feel like basking in the sun, I'd choose a saffron—very Indian and exotic-looking. But if I want to cut the brightness, I'd choose a dark, foresty brown."

GIL SCHAFER AND EVE ASHCRAFT
PRATT & LAMBERT | GUNNEL 25-23
Gil Shafer chose a smoky gray-blue paint for the floor. It
centers the room, absorbing the brightness of the walls
and windows while at the same time reflecting back a
warmth that adds a much-needed balancing effect to the
entire room.

MALCOLM KUTNER

DONALD KAUFMAN COLOR COLLECTION | DKC-28

"This is the color of light—sort of like crème fraîche and butter and sunlight and moonlight all mixed together. When it's sunshiny, it becomes more creamy, but when it's dark outside, it looks very bright and luminous."

MYRA HOEFER

FARROW & BALL | BONE 15

"You want something that kind of cools it down. This is the color of lichen on a tree, a gray-green that changes with the light. It's calming."

GARY MCBOURNIE

BENJAMIN MOORE | DAVENPORT TAN HC-76

"If a room is too bright, it gets all blown out and you stop seeing things. You want a color that absorbs light, like this dark, smoky brown. It makes me think of cigars and old sepia photographs."

BROOKE HUTTIG

SHERWIN-WILLIAMS | SHAGREEN SW6422

"My loggia faces south, so it's solid sun with white tile floors and a white-beamed ceiling. I glazed the walls with a sea-foamy green to counteract the heat and add a hint of water. Now it feels serene."

FROM THE GARDEN

Fruits, flowers, and foliage: from the deep indigo of eggplant to a morning glory's brilliant azure, nature is filled with lush colors. Borrow some of them for your own palette!

"This dining room has a very different feel; it's modern but with a bit of an ethnic mood. I want an almost sultry feeling. I pulled this deep plum color from this wonderfully rich David Hicks fabric."

ANGIE HRANOWKSY
PRATT & LAMBERT | JACK HORNER'S PLUM 1-20

OPPOSITE PAGE :

"I wanted that milky gray-green you see on lamb's ears, with an undertone of silver as the light hits it. Even in winter, it keeps that ethereal, dreamy feeling. One day, I'm going to find a place for the pink."

JAMES SWAN
PRATT & LAMBERT | PEARL WHITE 29-29 (TOP)
| ROSA LEE 1-13 (BOTTOM)

RANDALL BEALE

BENJAMIN MOORE | PEONY 2079-30

"Why not paint a powder room in the hot pink of a Gerber daisy? There's nothing more chic than hot pink walls with white marble floors."

MICHAEL WHALEY

BENJAMIN MOORE | CEDAR GROVE 444

"In my cutting garden I have morning glories climbing over a lattice obelisk painted this wonderful silvery sage green. It reminds me of lavender leaves."

KENNETH BROWN

BENJAMIN MOORE | STRAW 2154-50

"If you look into a calla lily, you'll see those little pollen stems in exactly this color—a golden yellow with a little apricot and peach to take off the edge."

In a Boston living room, designer James Swan
matched the color on the walls to the pale gray-green
of lamb's ears and painted the trim Pratt & Lambert
POR2343 FB.

DAN CARITHERS

BENJAMIN MOORE | BRAZILIAN BLUE 817

"Plumbago has tiny flowers, like phlox, and they're purplish blue, which has a cooling effect in a garden as well as a room. It's the prettiest color, so intense. An intense color can still be soft as long as it has a few shadows in it. This is a peaceful, late-evening blue."

....

ANN DUPUY

FARROW & BALL | PINK GROUND 202

"This is a very serene pink, the color of an old French rose called Cuisse de Nymphe, which translates as the thigh of a nymph. So charming. And everybody looks good against pink."

....

PATRICIA HEALING

BENJAMIN MOORE | FRENCH LILAC 1403

"My wisteria went absolutely crazy and gave me a whole new way of looking at lavender. Use this pale lilac with brown and white fabric, or navy blue. Very sophisticated."

....

S. RUSSELL GROVES

PRATT & LAMBERT | MOSS GREEN 16-29

"This is a great mossy green, very soft because of all the gray in it. There's nothing softer on bare feet than a carpet of moss. It feels like kitten fur."

KENDALL WILKINSON
BENJAMIN MOORE
| LINEN WHITE 70 (LEFT)
| JET STREAM 814 (RIGHT)
This is a cool shade that wavers between blue and lavender, a color you see in delphinium and hyacinth. It reads as blue on the wall, but the lilac undertones warm it up and make it more soothing.

On a sunny day, the walls are almost robin's egg blue. In the fog it turns a soft blue-gray.

AMY LAU

BENJAMIN MOORE | RUMBA ORANGE 2014-20

"It looks just like those dancing orange nasturtiums that climb and spill and ramble all over the garden. But I'd only use it in a low dose, as an accent color behind a bed or on a wall in a beach house, à la Barragán. Otherwise it would be overpowering."

WARM SHADES

A little of these colors goes a long way, so use them as accents and not on walls. Paint window frames, a door, a piece of furniture from the flea market, maybe even a bed frame—your room will come alive.

The surest way to freshen up a room is to borrow color straight from nature's infinite palette. With a bouquet of possibilities, the only difficult part comes in narrowing down the field. How can we pick just one?

Orange Lily
GLIDDEN
DESERT ORANGE
78YR39/593

Yellow Ranunculus
PRATT & LAMBERT
CANARY YELLOW 12-8

Red Rose
GLIDDEN
DRUM BEAT 00YR08/409

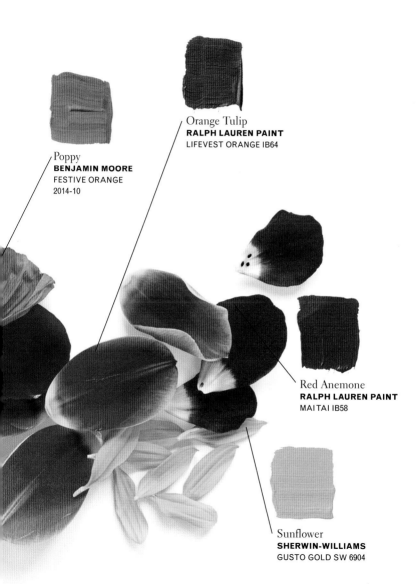

Poppy
BENJAMIN MOORE
FESTIVE ORANGE
2014-10

Orange Tulip
RALPH LAUREN PAINT
LIFEVEST ORANGE IB64

Red Anemone
RALPH LAUREN PAINT
MAI TAI IB58

Sunflower
SHERWIN-WILLIAMS
GUSTO GOLD SW 6904

COOL SHADES

A word about finishes. Light colors look darker in a flat finish. Dark colors look brighter in a gloss or semigloss. A flat finish will work well for the lighter shades here, but the deep purples and pinks will definitely look better with a sheen.

Hyacinth
PRATT & LAMBERT
ORIENTAL NIGHT 29-14

Orchid
GLIDDEN
VESPER 70RB67/067

Pink Rose
GLIDDEN
PEACHGLOW
90YR71/144

Pink Daisy
BENJAMIN MOORE
SMASHING PINK 1303

Water Lily
PRATT & LAMBERT
TULIPE VIOLET 30-14

Magenta Anemone
SHERWIN-WILLIAMS
FORWARD FUSCHIA
SW 6842

Peony
BENJAMIN MOORE
SWEET TAFFY 2086-60

Violet
BENJAMIN MOORE
GENTLE VIOLET
2071-20

Hydrangea
PRATT & LAMBERT
TROOPER 26-14

FOYER

BENJAMIN MOORE
NARRAGANSETT
GREEN HC-157

FARROW & BALL
LIGHT BLUE 22

**DONALD KAUFMAN
COLOR COLLECTION**
DKC-17

BENJAMIN MOORE
UTAH SKY 2065-40

BENJAMIN MOORE
BLUE SEAFOAM 2056-60

BENJAMIN MOORE
GRAYTINT 1611

BENJAMIN MOORE
SHOWTIME 923

BENJAMIN MOORE
IRON MOUNTAIN 2134-30

BENJAMIN MOORE
SALSA 2009-20

FOYER

FARROW & BALL
DRAB 41

BENJAMIN MOORE
PALLADIAN BLUE
HC-144

**FINE PAINTS
OF EUROPE**
DUTCH CHOCOLATE 6012

BENJAMIN MOORE
ELEPHANT TUSK OC-8

BENJAMIN MOORE
LINEN WHITE 70

RALPH LAUREN PAINT
RACER PINK 1B07

PRATT & LAMBERT
ARGENT 1322

BEHR'S DISNEY HOME
CLASSIC POOH
BUTTERFLY FLUTTER BY
DC2A-10-1

FARROW & BALL
FOLLY GREEN 76

FOYER

C2
QUAHOG 8385

**FINE PAINTS
OF EUROPE**
SPINNAKER WHITE 7032

BENJAMIN MOORE
SUMMER SHOWER 2135-60

**DONALD KAUFMAN
COLOR COLLECTION**
DKC-17

SHERWIN-WILLIAMS
STUDIO MAUVE 0062

BENJAMIN MOORE
GOLDEN STRAW 2152-50

SHERWIN-WILLIAMS
HAZEL 6471

C2
EXPEDITION 162

LIVING ROOM

BENJAMIN MOORE
COASTAL FOG AC-1

BENJAMIN MOORE
MAN ON THE MOON
OC-106

BENJAMIN MOORE
SUNDANCE 2022-50

C2
BELLA DONNA C2-316 W

FARROW & BALL
BISCUIT 38

BENJAMIN MOORE
CORAL SPICE 2170-40

FARROW & BALL
COOKING APPLE
GREEN 32

BENJAMIN MOORE
ICEBERG 2122-50

SHERWIN-WILLIAMS
VERDITER BLUE
DCR078 NRH

LIVING ROOM

BENJAMIN MOORE
AQUARIUS 788

BENJAMIN MOORE
MORNING SUNSHINE
2018-50

BENJAMIN MOORE
ONYX 2133-10

BENJAMIN MOORE
HORIZON GRAY 2141-50

BENJAMIN MOORE
SADDLE SOAP 2110-30

BENJAMIN MOORE
TUDOR BROWN

BENJAMIN MOORE
LADYBUG RED 1322

BENJAMIN MOORE
SHENANDOAH TAUPE
AC-36

BENJAMIN MOORE
LAVENDER ICE 2069-60

LIVING ROOM

SHERWIN-WILLIAMS
LEAPFROG 6431

PRATT & LAMBERT
VINTAGE CLARET 1013

BENJAMIN MOORE
RUBY RED 2001-10

BENJAMIN MOORE
POWELL BUFF HC-35

RALPH LAUREN PAINT
CALIFORNIA POPPY
GH170

C2
ENOKI 425

RALPH LAUREN PAINT
YELLOWHAMMER GH100

PORTER PAINTS
PERSIAN PINK 6650-1

BENJAMIN MOORE
SMOKE EMBERS 1466

COLOR INDEX *Room by Room*

LIVING ROOM

PRATT & LAMBERT
ROSA LEE 1-13

BENJAMIN MOORE
STRAW 2154-50

BENJAMIN MOORE
FRENCH LILAC 1403

DINING ROOM

BENJAMIN MOORE
DARK ROYAL BLUE 2065-20

BENJAMIN MOORE
SUNDANCE 2022-50

FARROW & BALL
SHADED WHITE 201

DINING ROOM

C2
SORCERER 5326

PARKER PAINT
WATERSIDE 7573M

RALPH LAUREN PAINT
MASTER ROOM VM99

BENJAMIN MOORE
HEPPLEWHITE IVORY
HC-36

FARROW & BALL
BREAKFAST ROOM
GREEN 81

BENJAMIN MOORE
BRANCHPORT BROWN
HC-72

FARROW & BALL
MERE GREEN 219

BENJAMIN MOORE
ORANGE PARROT 2169-20

BENJAMIN MOORE
WISPY GREEN 414

DINING ROOM

RALPH LAUREN PAINT
CALYPSO VM138

BENJAMIN MOORE
SAGE TINT 458

BENJAMIN MOORE
CHOCOLATE CANDY
BROWN 2107-10

BENJAMIN MOORE
ATRIUM WHITE INT. RM

BENJAMIN MOORE
SHELBURNE BUFF HC-28

BENJAMIN MOORE
POWDER SAND 2151-70

RALPH LAUREN PAINT
DESERT BOOT TH35

BENJAMIN MOORE
BROWN SUGAR 112-20

BENJAMIN MOORE
REDSTONE 2009-10

COLOR INDEX *Room by Room*

DINING ROOM

GLIDDEN
CHECKERBERRY
32RR50/260

BENJAMIN MOORE
TUCSON RED 1300

FARROW & BALL
ORANGERY 70

DUNN-EDWARDS
DEEP CARNATION DE5011

BENJAMIN MOORE
MOROCCAN RED 1309

PRATT & LAMBERT
JACK HORNER'S
PLUM 1-20

FARROW & BALL
CLUNCH 2009

**DONALD KAUFMAN
COLOR COLLECTION**
DKC-66

FARROW & BALL
MINSTER GREEN 224

BENJAMIN MOORE
GLASS SLIPPER 1632

BENJAMIN MOORE
PATRIOT BLUE 2064-20

BENJAMIN MOORE
DEEP TAUPE 2111-10

FARROW & BALL
COOKING APPLE
GREEN 32

BENJAMIN MOORE
MERLOT RED 2006-10

FARROW & BALL
CLAYDON BLUE 87

MARTIN SENOUR
MARKET SQUARE TAVERN
DARK GREEN CW401

BENJAMIN MOORE
ALLIGATOR ALLEY 441

FARROW & BALL
RADICCHIO 96

BENJAMIN MOORE
GREAT BARRINGTON
GREEN HC-122

BENJAMIN MOORE
ARUBA BLUE 2048-30

BENJAMIN MOORE
CORAL GABLES 2010-40

KITCHEN

PRATT & LAMBERT
SILVER BLOND 14-29

FARROW & BALL
DOWN PIPE 26

PRATT & LAMBERT
FLINT 32-20

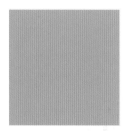

BENJAMIN MOORE
WEDGEWOOD GRAY
HC-146

BENJAMIN MOORE
WOODLAWN BLUE HC-147

BENJAMIN MOORE
WARM SIENNA 1203

BENJAMIN MOORE
GOLDEN HONEY 297

SHERWIN-WILLIAMS
WHOLE WHEAT SW6121

**FINE PAINTS
OF EUROPE**
P11130

COLOR INDEX *Room by Room*

KITCHEN

BENJAMIN MOORE
SCARECROW 1041

BENJAMIN MOORE
RAZZLE DAZZLE 1348

RALPH LAUREN PAINT
CREAM STONE UL54

RALPH LAUREN PAINT
WEATHERED BROWN
UL44

VALSPAR
SPRING SQUASH 2008-1B

BENJAMIN MOORE
MERLOT RED 2006-10

BENJAMIN MOORE
WOLF GRAY 2127-40

PRATT & LAMBERT
TAMPICO 1411

BENJAMIN MOORE
GREAT BARRINGTON
GREEN HC-122

KITCHEN

**DONALD KAUFMAN
COLOR COLLECTION**
DKC-23

BENJAMIN MOORE
PINK CORSAGE 1349

BATHROOM

SHERWIN-WILLIAMS
PALE EARTH 8133

FARROW & BALL
LIGHT BLUE 22

BENJAMIN MOORE
RED PARROT 1308

BATHROOM

PRATT & LAMBERT
COOS BAY 19-31

BENJAMIN MOORE
BRILLIANT WHITE

PRATT & LAMBERT
ANTIQUE WHITE 2207

BENJAMIN MOORE
CALIFORNIA BLUE 2060-20

PRATT & LAMBERT
AUTUMN CROCUS 1141

RALPH LAUREN
ARCHITECTURAL
CREAM UL 55

PRATT & LAMBERT
SILVER BIRCH 18-31

PRATT & LAMBERT
SOLITARY 19-29

FARROW & BALL
DIMITY 2008

BATHROOM

BENJAMIN MOORE
TANGERINE DREAM
2012-30

**DONALD KAUFMAN
COLOR COLLECTION**
DKC-64

BENJAMIN MOORE
SILVER SATIN OC-26

BENJAMIN MOORE
CARRINGTON BEIGE
HC-93

SHERWIN-WILLIAMS
BRAINSTORM BRONZE
7033

BENJAMIN MOORE
FRESH DEW 435

FARROW & BALL
YELLOW GROUND 218

PRATT & LAMBERT
WENDIGO 2293

PRATT & LAMBERT
PELHAM GRAY LIGHT
CW 819

BATHROOM

**FINE PAINTS
OF EUROPE**
DUTCHLAC BRILLIANT
TULIP RED W1001B-M

PRATT & LAMBERT
PAGODA RED 5-15

BENJAMIN MOORE
FLORIDA PINK 1320

BENJAMIN MOORE
PEONY 2079-30

BEDROOM

BENJAMIN MOORE
SILKEN PINE 2144-50

BENJAMIN MOORE
CORAL REEF 012

FARROW & BALL
BORROWED LIGHT 235

BENJAMIN MOORE
MORNING GLORY 785

FARROW & BALL
MATCHSTICK 2013

BEHR
PLANTATION WHITE
WN-18

C2
BELLA DONNA C2-316W

FARROW & BALL
PALE HOUND 71

BENJAMIN MOORE
STARRY NIGHT BLUE
2067-20

BEDROOM

SHERWIN-WILLIAMS
BLUE HUBBARD 8438

BENJAMIN MOORE
COLONY GREEN 694

BENJAMIN MOORE
BLUE WAVE 2065 -50

BENJAMIN MOORE
SEAPEARL OC-19

BENJAMIN MOORE
HOLIDAY WREATH 447

BENJAMIN MOORE
MISTY LILAC 2071-70

FARROW & BALL
BORROWED LIGHT 235

PRATT & LAMBERT
AVOINE DE MER 17-26

BENJAMIN MOORE
PALE MOON OC-108

BEDROOM

BENJAMIN MOORE
SUN-KISSED YELLOW
2022-20

RALPH LAUREN PAINT
CRESTED BUTTE NA40

BENJAMIN MOORE
BLANCHED CORAL 886

FARROW & BALL
GREEN BLUE 84

BENJAMIN MOORE
CAYMAN BLUE 2060-50

GLIDDEN
LIMOGES BLUE 30BG56/045

**DONALD KAUFMAN
COLOR COLLECTION**
DKC-37

C2
BELLA DONNA C2-316

FARROW & BALL
CITRON 74

BEDROOM

BENJAMIN MOORE
BIRD'S EGG 2051-60

BENJAMIN MOORE
RIVIERA AZURE 822

BENJAMIN MOORE
RED 2000-10

BENJAMIN MOORE
VALLEY FORGE BROWN
HC-74

BENJAMIN MOORE
MUSTANG 2111-30

BENJAMIN MOORE
MADISON AVENUE 759

BENJAMIN MOORE
CHILI PEPPER 2004-20

**FINE PAINTS
OF EUROPE**
COLONIAL ROSE 7102T

SHERWIN-WILLIAMS
BAGEL 6114

BEDROOM

BENJAMIN MOORE
MIDNIGHT NAVY 2067-10

BENJAMIN MOORE
OPAL ESSENCE 680

PORTER PAINTS
PARSLEY TINT 6998-1

BENJAMIN MOORE
QUEEN ANNE PINK HC-60

BENJAMIN MOORE
VAN BUREN BROWN
HC-70

BENJAMIN MOORE
JET STREAM 814

COLOR INDEX *Shade by Shade*

WHITE

BENJAMIN MOORE
SUPER WHITE INT. RM

DONALD KAUFMAN COLOR COLLECTION
DKC-51

BENJAMIN MOORE
DECORATOR'S WHITE INT. RM

RALPH LAUREN PAINT
POCKET WATCH WHITE WW11

FARROW & BALL
ALL WHITE 2005

BENJAMIN MOORE
ACADIA WHITE OC-38

BENJAMIN MOORE
IVORY WHITE 925

FINE PAINTS OF EUROPE
SPINNAKER WHITE 7032

PRATT & LAMBERT
SEED PEARL 27-32

WHITE

BENJAMIN MOORE
SILVER SATIN OC-26

BENJAMIN MOORE
WINTER WHITE 2140-70

**DONALD KAUFMAN
COLOR COLLECTION**
DKC-5

PRATT & LAMBERT
ANTIQUE WHITE 2207

BENJAMIN MOORE
BRILLIANT WHITE

FARROW & BALL
STRONG WHITE 2001

BENJAMIN MOORE
CHINA WHITE INT. RM

FARROW & BALL
POINTING 2003

BENJAMIN MOORE
MAN ON THE MOON
OC-106

CREAM—PALE TAN

BENJAMIN MOORE
LINEN WHITE INT. RM. 70

BENJAMIN MOORE
SWISS COFFEE OC-45

BENJAMIN MOORE
ALABASTER OC-129

BENJAMIN MOORE
POWDER SAND 2151-70

**DONALD KAUFMAN
COLOR COLLECTION**
DKC-28

FARROW & BALL
TALLOW 203

FARROW & BALL
MATCHSTICK 2013

BENJAMIN MOORE
ATRIUM WHITE INT. RM

**FULL SPECTRUM
PAINTS**
MUSHROOM

TAN—GRAY

BENJAMIN MOORE
QUEEN ANNE PINK HC-60

BENJAMIN MOORE
WHITE CHOCOLATE
OC-127

PRATT & LAMBERT
SILVER LINING 32-32

FARROW & BALL
SLIPPER SATIN 2004

BENJAMIN MOORE
SILKEN PINE 2144-50

RALPH LAUREN PAINT
ARCHITECTURAL
CREAM UL 55

**DONALD KAUFMAN
COLOR COLLECTION**
DKC-54

**OLD FASHIONED MILK
PAINT CO.**
OYSTER WHITE

BENJAMIN MOORE
HORIZON 1478

TAN—GRAY

PRATT & LAMBERT
PEARL WHITE 29-29

BENJAMIN MOORE
GRANT BEIGE HC-83

PRATT & LAMBERT
FRESH CREAM 11-5

BENJAMIN MOORE
COASTAL FOG AC-1

FARROW & BALL
BONE 15

BENJAMIN MOORE
BLEEKER BEIGE HC-80

BENJAMIN MOORE
SMOKEY TAUPE 983

PRATT & LAMBERT
PELHAM GRAY LIGHT
CW-819

SHERWIN-WILLIAMS
HONIED WHITE 7106

BEIGE

BENJAMIN MOORE
WINDHAM CREAM HG-6

FULL SPECTRUM PAINTS
BUTTERCREAM

BENJAMIN MOORE
STRAW 2154-50

RALPH LAUREN COLOR COLLECTION
YELLOWHAMMER GH100

SHERWIN-WILLIAMS
IVOIRE SW6127

FARROW & BALL
PALE HOUND 71

SHERWIN-WILLIAMS
HUMBLE GOLD SW6380

PRATT & LAMBERT
AVOINE DE MER 17-26

BENJAMIN MOORE
POWELL BUFF HC-35

BEIGE

BENJAMIN MOORE
HEPPLEWHITE IVORY
HC-36

RALPH LAUREN PAINT
CREAM STONE UL54

BENJAMIN MOORE
LAVENDER ICE 2069-60

C2
ENOKI 425

BENJAMIN MOORE
MORNING SUNSHINE
2018-50

**PHILIP'S
PERFECT COLORS**
AGUA VERTE PPC-BL7

**FINE PAINTS
OF EUROPE**
LP-16

SHERWIN-WILLIAMS
PALE EARTH 8133

C2
CHAI 7293

BROWN

FARROW & BALL
STRING 8

SHERWIN-WILLIAMS
WHOLE WHEAT SW6121

BENJAMIN MOORE
PAPAYA 957

BENJAMIN MOORE
SHELBURNE BUFF HC-28

SHERWIN-WILLIAMS
BAGEL 6114

PRATT & LAMBERT
SILVER BLOND 14-29

FARROW & BALL
CLUNCH 2009

C2
CAFÉ LATTE 7314

PRATT & LAMBERT
SOLITARY 19-29

BROWN

BENJAMIN MOORE
CAMEL BACK 1103

FARROW & BALL
BISCUIT 38

BENJAMIN MOORE
VALLEY FORGE BROWN
HC-74

RALPH LAUREN PAINT
CRESTED BUTTE NA40

BENJAMIN MOORE
SEAPEARL OC-19

**DONALD KAUFMAN
COLOR COLLECTION**
DKC-64

C2
QUAHOG 8385

FARROW & BALL
DRAB 41

BENJAMIN MOORE
DANVILLE TAN HC-91

BROWN

PRATT & LAMBERT
GLOAMING 2145

PRATT & LAMBERT
FLINT 32-20

BENJAMIN MOORE
CARRINGTON BEIGE
HC-93

RALPH LAUREN PAINT
MASTER ROOM VM99

PRATT & LAMBERT
SILVER BIRCH 18-31

BENJAMIN MOORE
WHITALL BROWN HC-69

BENJAMIN MOORE
SCARECROW 1041

**PHILIP'S PERFECT
COLORS**
MINK PPC-G13

RALPH LAUREN PAINT
WEATHERED BROWN
UL44

BROWN

BENJAMIN MOORE
DAVENPORT TAN HC-76

BENJAMIN MOORE
SHENANDOAH TAUPE
AC-36

DUNN-EDWARDS
COCONUT SKIN DE1055

BENJAMIN MOORE
SADDLE SOAP 2110-30

BENJAMIN MOORE
NORTH CREEK
BROWN 1001

BENJAMIN MOORE
DECK ENAMEL RICH
BROWN 60

BENJAMIN MOORE
BRANCHPORT BROWN
HC-72

BENJAMIN MOORE
ONYX 2133-10

BENJAMIN MOORE
MUSTANG 2111-30

BROWN

BENJAMIN MOORE
BROWN SUGAR 2112-20

PRATT & LAMBERT
WENDIGO 2293

BENJAMIN MOORE
VAN BUREN BROWN
HC-70

RALPH LAUREN PAINT
DESERT BOOT TH35

BENJAMIN MOORE
CHOCOLATE CANDY
BROWN 2107-10

FARROW & BALL
MAHOGANY 36

**DONALD KAUFMAN
COLOR COLLECTION**
DKC-66

BENJAMIN MOORE
WENGE AF-180

BENJAMIN MOORE
DEEP TAUPE 2111-10

BROWN

**FINE PAINTS
OF EUROPE**
DUTCH CHOCOLATE 6012

BENJAMIN MOORE
TUDOR BROWN

SHERWIN-WILLIAMS
BRAINSTORM BRONZE
7033

YELLOW

BENJAMIN MOORE
PALE MOON OC-108

BENJAMIN MOORE
GOLDEN STRAW 2152-50

**DONALD KAUFMAN
COLOR COLLECTION**
DKC-30

BENJAMIN MOORE
GOLDEN HONEY 297

BENJAMIN MOORE
SUNDANCE 2022-50

BENJAMIN MOORE
DALILA 319

RALPH LAUREN PAINT
GOLDFINCH GH105

BENJAMIN MOORE
LITTLE ANGEL 318

**FINE PAINTS
OF EUROPE**
SUNNYSIDE LANE 7014T

YELLOW

BENJAMIN MOORE
SUN-KISSED YELLOW
2022-20

PRATT & LAMBERT
CANARY YELLOW 12-8

GLIDDEN
YELLOW GOLD 758

FARROW & BALL
YELLOW GROUND 218

BENJAMIN MOORE
SHOWTIME 923

FARROW & BALL
CITRON 74

FARROW & BALL
BABOUCHE 223

FARROW & BALL
CIARA YELLOW 73

**DONALD KAUFMAN
COLOR COLLECTION**
DKC-20

ORANGE

SHERWIN-WILLIAMS
GUSTO GOLD SW 6904

GLIDDEN
DESERT ORANGE
78YR39/593

VALSPAR
SPRING SQUASH 2008-1B

FARROW & BALL
ORANGERY 70

BENJAMIN MOORE
CITRUS BLAST 2018-30

BENJAMIN MOORE
SOFT PUMPKIN 2166-40

BEHR
YAM 290B-7

SHERWIN-WILLIAMS
SUNFLOWER SW 6678

BENJAMIN MOORE
CALYPSO ORANGE
2015-30

COLOR INDEX *Shade by Shade*

ORANGE

RALPH LAUREN PAINT
CALIFORNIA POPPY
GH170

PHILIP'S PERFECT COLORS
ADOBE O8

SHERWIN-WILLIAMS
DETERMINED ORANGE
6635

BENJAMIN MOORE
TANGERINE FUSION 083

PRATT & LAMBERT
NASTURTIUM 1830

BENJAMIN MOORE
RUMBA ORANGE 2014-20

BENJAMIN MOORE
FESTIVE ORANGE 2014-10

BENJAMIN MOORE
TANGERINE DREAM
2012-30

BENJAMIN MOORE
ORANGE PARROT
2169-20

PINK

RALPH LAUREN PAINT
WALTON CREAM VM65

FARROW & BALL
DIMITY 2008

FARROW & BALL
PINK GROUND 202

BENJAMIN MOORE
BLANCHED CORAL 886

BENJAMIN MOORE
SMASHING PINK 1303

GLIDDEN
PEACHGLOW 90YR71/144

BENJAMIN MOORE
SWEET TAFFY 2086-60

BENJAMIN MOORE
ROMANTIC PINK 2004-70

GLIDDEN
CHECKERBERRY
32RR50/260

PINK

PORTER PAINTS
PERSIAN PINK 6650-1

GLIDDEN
VESPER 70RB67/067

PORTOLA PAINTS
GERANIUM 005

BENJAMIN MOORE
PEONY 2079-30

SHERWIN-WILLIAMS
FORWARD FUSCHIA
SW 6842

BENJAMIN MOORE
PINK CORSAGE 1349

RALPH LAUREN PAINT
RACER PINK 1B07

BENJAMIN MOORE
RAZZLE DAZZLE 1348

BENJAMIN MOORE
MILANO RED 1313

PINK

BEHR
CANDY COATED 120B-5

SHERWIN-WILLIAMS
IN THE PINK SW 6583

FINE PAINTS OF EUROPE
COLONIAL ROSE 7102T

BENJAMIN MOORE
OLD WORLD 2011-40

BENJAMIN MOORE
RED PARROT 1308

BENJAMIN MOORE
CORAL GABLES 2010-40

BENJAMIN MOORE
CORAL PINK 2003-50

FARROW & BALL
FOWLER PINK 39

BENJAMIN MOORE
CORAL REEF 012

PINK

BENJAMIN MOORE
CORAL SPICE 2170-40

BENJAMIN MOORE
FLORIDA PINK 1320

RED

FARROW & BALL
MENAGERIE 63

**FINE PAINTS
OF EUROPE**
WINTERSWEET BERRY
5104T

**PAPERS AND
PAINTS LTD.**
MOORISH RED HC55

RED

PORTOLA PAINTS
PAPRIKA 013

BENJAMIN MOORE
WARM SIENNA 1203

FARROW & BALL
BLAZER 212

RALPH LAUREN PAINT
MAITAI IB58

RALPH LAUREN PAINT
LIFEVEST ORANGE IB64

BENJAMIN MOORE
RED 2000-10

BENJAMIN MOORE
RUBY RED 2001-10

RALPH LAUREN PAINT
LATTICE RED IB57

**FINE PAINTS
OF EUROPE**
DUTCHLAC BRILLIANT
TULIP RED W1001B-M

RED

BENJAMIN MOORE
SALSA 2009-20

BENJAMIN MOORE
REDSTONE 2009-10

PRATT & LAMBERT
VINTAGE CLARET 1013

PRATT & LAMBERT
SCARLET O'HARA 1870

BENJAMIN MOORE
HERITAGE RED EXT. RM.

BENJAMIN MOORE
LADYBUG RED 1322

BENJAMIN MOORE
CHILI PEPPER 2004-20

BENJAMIN MOORE
MOROCCAN RED 1309

FARROW & BALL
RECTORY RED 217

RED

BENJAMIN MOORE
MILLION DOLLAR RED
2003-10

BENJAMIN MOORE
MERLOT RED 2006-10

PRATT & LAMBERT
PAGODA RED 5-15

BENJAMIN MOORE
TUCSON RED 1300

RALPH LAUREN PAINT
DRESSAGE RED TH41

RALPH LAUREN PAINT
RELAY RED IB11

BENJAMIN MOORE
SANGRIA 2006-20

**DONALD KAUFMAN
COLOR COLLECTION**
DKC-17

FARROW & BALL
PICTURE GALLERY
RED 42

RED

BENJAMIN MOORE
RUST 2175-30

GLIDDEN
DRUM BEAT 00YR08/409

GREEN

RALPH LAUREN PAINT
BASALT VM121

BENJAMIN MOORE
SWEET DREAMS 847

BENJAMIN MOORE
OPAL ESSENCE 680

BENJAMIN MOORE
FRESH DEW 435

BENJAMIN MOORE
WISPY GREEN 414

**DURON MOUNT
VERNON ESTATE OF
COLOURS**
LEAMON SIRRUP DMV070

PORTER PAINTS
PARSLEY TINT 6998-1

BENJAMIN MOORE
PALE VISTA 2029-60

DUNN-EDWARDS
PERFECT PEAR DE5519

GREEN

BENJAMIN MOORE
LEMON FREEZE 2025-50

BENJAMIN MOORE
CHIC LIME 396

PRATT & LAMBERT
MOSS GREEN 16-29

**DONALD KAUFMAN
COLOR COLLECTION**
DKC-11

**FINE PAINTS
OF EUROPE**
P11130

BENJAMIN MOORE
POTPOURRI GREEN
2029-50

SHERWIN-WILLIAMS
SHAGREEN SW6422

BENJAMIN MOORE
FERNWOOD GREEN
2145-40

FARROW & BALL
GREEN GROUND 206

COLOR INDEX *Shade by Shade*

GREEN

FARROW & BALL
COOKING APPLE
GREEN 32

C2
SALTY BRINE C2-4388

PRATT & LAMBERT
TAMPICO 1411

**DONALD KAUFMAN
COLOR COLLECTION**
DKC-23

ROLLINSON HUES
31

KELLY-MOORE
CACTUS CAFÉ KM3431-3

FARROW & BALL
FOLLY GREEN 76

**FINE PAINTS
OF EUROPE**
2030-G70Y

FARROW & BALL
BREAKFAST ROOM
GREEN 81

GREEN

BENJAMIN MOORE
SEA FOAM 2123-60

BENJAMIN MOORE
MADISON AVENUE 759

BENJAMIN MOORE
ARUBA BLUE 2048-30

RALPH LAUREN PAINT
OYSTER BAY SS61

FARROW & BALL
MERE GREEN 219

SHERWIN-WILLIAMS
LEAPFROG 6431

C2
EXPEDITION 162

BENJAMIN MOORE
GREAT BARRINGTON
GREEN HC-122

BENJAMIN MOORE
ALLIGATOR ALLEY 441

GREEN

BENJAMIN MOORE
GARDEN CUCUMBER 644

PRATT & LAMBERT
DEEP JUNGLE 21-17

DUNN-EDWARDS
AFTER THE STORM
DE5769

FARROW & BALL
MINSTER GREEN 224

BENJAMIN MOORE
DEEP RIVER 1582

MARTIN SENOUR
MARKET SQUARE TAVERN
DARK GREEN CW401

BENJAMIN MOORE
ESSEX GREEN EXT. RM

GRAY—GREEN

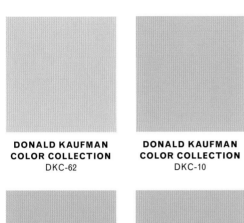

**DONALD KAUFMAN
COLOR COLLECTION**
DKC-62

**DONALD KAUFMAN
COLOR COLLECTION**
DKC-10

BENJAMIN MOORE
SOFT FERN 2144-40

FARROW & BALL
VERT DE TERRE 234

BENJAMIN MOORE
MESQUITE 501

BENJAMIN MOORE
RACCOON HOLLOW 978

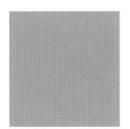

FARROW & BALL
SHADED WHITE 201

BEHR
PLANTATION WHITE
WN-18

**DONALD KAUFMAN
COLOR COLLECTION**
DKC-8

GRAY

BENJAMIN MOORE
SMOKE EMBERS 1466

RALPH LAUREN PAINT
LINEN UL03

BENJAMIN MOORE
STONE HARBOR 2111-50

BENJAMIN MOORE
COLOR COLLECTION
ELEPHANT TUSK OC-8

BENJAMIN MOORE
HORIZON GRAY 2141-50

BENJAMIN MOORE
NANTUCKET GRAY
HC-111

BENJAMIN MOORE
NOVEMBER RAIN 2142-60

SHERWIN-WILLIAMS
MAGNETIC GRAY
SW-7058

FARROW & BALL
LIGHT BLUE 22

BLUE—GRAY

PRATT & LAMBERT
ARGENT 1322

BENJAMIN MOORE
COLONY GREEN 694

BENJAMIN MOORE
HEAVENLY BLUE 709

FARROW & BALL
GREEN BLUE 84

BENJAMIN MOORE
SAGE TINT 458

BENJAMIN MOORE
WOODLAWN BLUE
HC-147

BENJAMIN MOORE
PALLADIAN BLUE HC-144

BENJAMIN MOORE
WEDGEWOOD GRAY
HC-146

SHERWIN-WILLIAMS
HAZEL 6471

BLUE—GREEN

BENJAMIN MOORE
CEDAR GROVE 444

PRATT & LAMBERT
PERIDOT 18-20

BENJAMIN MOORE
BUXTON BLUE HC-149

PRATT & LAMBERT
COOS BAY 19-31

BENJAMIN MOORE
BLUE SEAFOAM 2056-60

BENJAMIN MOORE
ICEBERG 2122-50

BENJAMIN MOORE
SEA STAR 2123-30

BENJAMIN MOORE
MISTY MEMORIES 2118-60

RALPH LAUREN PAINT
BLUE-GREEN GH81

DARK GRAY

**OLD FASHIONED
MILK PAINT CO.**
SLATE

BENJAMIN MOORE
GRAYTINT 1611

BENJAMIN MOORE
BEAR CREEK 1470

GLIDDEN
ICON GREY 1677

FARROW & BALL
DOWN PIPE 26

BENJAMIN MOORE
WOLF GRAY 2127-40

PRATT & LAMBERT
GUNNEL 25-23

BENJAMIN MOORE
HOLIDAY WREATH 447

FARROW & BALL
CLAYDON BLUE 87

DARK GRAY

SHERWIN-WILLIAMS
BLUE HUBBARD 8438

BENJAMIN MOORE
IRON MOUNTAIN 2134-30

BENJAMIN MOORE
DECK ENAMEL BLACK
C-112-80

BLUE

BENJAMIN MOORE
PATRIOTIC WHITE 2135-70

BENJAMIN MOORE
ICY BLUE 2057-70

BENJAMIN MOORE
STONINGTON GRAY
HC-170

BLUE

FARROW & BALL
BORROWED LIGHT 235

BENJAMIN MOORE
WHITE SATIN 2067-70

BENJAMIN MOORE
BLUE ANGEL 2058-70

BENJAMIN MOORE
JAMAICAN AQUA 2048-60

RALPH LAUREN PAINT
PRUSSIAN BLUE VM122

BENJAMIN MOORE
LOOKOUT POINT 1646

**DONALD KAUFMAN
COLOR COLLECTION**
DKC-37

BENJAMIN MOORE
GLASS SLIPPER 1632

BENJAMIN MOORE
SUMMER SHOWER 2135-60

BLUE

BENJAMIN MOORE
BIRD'S EGG 2051-60

BENJAMIN MOORE
MORNING GLORY 785

FARROW & BALL
BLUE GROUND 210

SHERWIN-WILLIAMS
VERDITER BLUE
DCR078 NRH

BENJAMIN MOORE
COOL AQUA 2056-40

PARKER PAINT
WATERSIDE 7573M

BENJAMIN MOORE
AQUARIUS 788

BENJAMIN MOORE
CAYMAN BLUE 2060-50

BENJAMIN MOORE
BLUE WAVE 2065 -50

BLUE

FARROW & BALL
CHINESE BLUE 90

BENJAMIN MOORE
BLUE BELLE 782

BENJAMIN MOORE
UTAH SKY 2065-40

BENJAMIN MOORE
CLEAREST OCEAN BLUE
2064-40

MODERN MASTERS
VENETIAN BLUE ME-429

BENJAMIN MOORE
PADDINGTON BLUE
791

PRATT & LAMBERT
WINDSOR BLUE 27-19

BENJAMIN MOORE
SANTA MONICA BLUE 776

PORTOLA PAINTS
BLUE CART 094

BLUE

C2
ELECTRIC 275

BENJAMIN MOORE
CALIFORNIA BLUE
2060-20

BENJAMIN MOORE
PATRIOT BLUE 2064-20

BENJAMIN MOORE
DARK ROYAL BLUE
2065-20

PRATT & LAMBERT
BLUEBERRY MYRTILLE
1208-3

C2
SORCERER 5326

BENJAMIN MOORE
STARRY NIGHT BLUE
2067-20

BENJAMIN MOORE
MIDNIGHT NAVY 2067-10

BENJAMIN MOORE
CARBON COPY 2117-10

PURPLE

BENJAMIN MOORE
MISTY LILAC 2071-70

BENJAMIN MOORE
SPRING IRIS 1402

SHERWIN-WILLIAMS
STUDIO MAUVE 0062

GLIDDEN
LIMOGES BLUE 30BG56/045

BEHR'S DISNEY HOME
CLASSIC POOH
BUTTERFLY FLUTTER BY
DC2A-10-1

BENJAMIN MOORE
PEACE AND HAPPINESS
1380

C2
BELLA DONNA C2-316W

BENJAMIN MOORE
WINDMILL WINGS 2067-60

SHERWIN-WILLIAMS
SASSY BLUE 1241

PURPLE

BENJAMIN MOORE
JET STREAM 814

BENJAMIN MOORE
FRENCH LILAC 1403

BENJAMIN MOORE
ORIENTAL IRIS 1418

BENJAMIN MOORE
RIVIERA AZURE 822

PRATT & LAMBERT
AUTUMN CROCUS 1141

BENJAMIN MOORE
PERSIAN VIOLET 1419

BENJAMIN MOORE
SUMMER BLUE 2067-50

BENJAMIN MOORE
BRAZILIAN BLUE 817

PRATT & LAMBERT
TROOPER 26-14

PURPLE

RALPH LAUREN PAINT
CALYPSO VM138

PRATT & LAMBERT
TULIPE VIOLET 30-14

PRATT & LAMBERT
ROSA LEE 1-13

DUNN-EDWARDS
DEEP CARNATION DE5011

PRATT & LAMBERT
ORIENTAL NIGHT 29-14

BENJAMIN MOORE
GENTLE VIOLET 2071-20

PRATT & LAMBERT
JACK HORNER'S PLUM
1-20

BENJAMIN MOORE
MYSTICAL GRAPE 2071-30

BENJAMIN MOORE
GRAPPA 1393

DESIGNER INDEX

INDEX KEY

BM — Benjamin Moore
BR — Behr
DE — Dunn-Edwards
DKC — Donald Kaufman Color Collection
FB — Farrow & Ball
FPE — Fine Paints of Europe
FSP — Full Spectrum Paints
GL — Glidden
OFM — Old Fashioned Milk Paint Co.
PL — Pratt & Lambert
PPC — Philip's Perfect Color
RLP — Ralph Lauren Paint
SW — Sherwin-Williams

Jonathan Adler
    Pocket Watch White WW11 by RLP, 37
Kim Alexandriuk
    Babouche 223 by FB, 155
DD Allen
    Bella Donna C2-316 W by C2, 38, 39, 114
    Sorcerer 5326 by C2, 52
    Venetian Blue ME-429 by Modern Masters, 148
Eve Ashcraft and Gil Schafer
    Fresh Cream 11-5 by PL, 181
    Narragansett Green HC-157 by BM, 15
    Peridot 18-20 by PL, 148, 149
    Stonington Gray HC-170 by BM, 15
    Windsor Blue 27-19 by PL, 181
Anthony Baratta and William Diamond
    Essex Green Ext. Rm by BM, 155
    Lattice Red 1B57 by RLP, 133
    Sassy Blue 1241 by SW, 60
John Barman
    Racer Pink 1B07 by RLP, 71
Barbara Barry
    DKC-8 by DKC, 51
Dan Barsanti
    Alligator Alley 441 by BM, 162
Randall Beale
    Peony 2079-30 by BM, 200
Ruby Beets
    Smoke Embers 1466 by BM, 193
Brett Beldock
    Grappa 1393 by BM, 160
Jason Bell
    Hepplewhite Ivory HC-36 by BM, 102, 103
    Ladybug Red 1322 by BM, 80
    Saddle Soap 2110-30 by BM, 80

Tampico 1411 by PL, 91
    Tudor Brown by BM, 80
Robin Bell
    Dimity 2008 by FB, 97
    Paddington Blue 791 by BM, 64
Sara Bengur
    Blue Ground 210 by FB, 180
    DKC-20 by DKC, 50
    DKC-30 by DKC, 122
Michael Berman
    Desert Boot TH35 by RLP, 107
    Perfect Pear DE5519 by DE, 195
Bruce Bierman
    Autumn Crocus 1141 by PL, 152
Jeffrey Bilhuber
    Pale Vista 2029-60 by BM, 45
    Peace and Happiness 1380 by BM, 46
    2030-G70Y by FPE, 179
    Wispy Green 414 by BM, 104
Stephen Brady
    Bagel 6114 by SW, 172, 173
Nancy Braithwaite
    Pearly Gates 2268 by PL, 193
    Van Buren Brown HC-70 by BM, 48, 194
Alessandra Branca
    Avoine de Mer 17-26 by PL, 111
    DKC-23 by DKC, 146
Gerrie Bremermann
    Papaya 957 by BM, 45
    Raccoon Hollow 978 by BM, 48
Ronald Bricke
    Autumn Crocus 1141 by PL, 95
Sheila Bridges
    Green Blue 84 by FB, 112
Tom Britt
    Spinnaker White 7032 by FPE, 75
Betsy Brown
    Silver Lining 32-32 by PL, 31
    Wendigo 2293 by PL, 99
Kenneth Brown
    Straw 2154-50 by BM, 200
Mario Buatta
    Great Barrington Green HC-122 by BM, 169
    Merlot Red 2006-10 by BM, 129
    Misty Lilac 2071-70 by BM, 111
    Sundance 2022-50 by BM, 28
    Windham Cream HC-6 by BM, 156
Thomas Burak
    Heritage Red Ext. Rm by BM, 155

Barclay Butera
    Calypso VM138 by RLP, 104
    Cream Stone UL54 by RLP, 88
    Weathered Brown UL44 by RLP, 88
Libby Cameron
    Milano Red 1313 by BM, 120, 121
Dan Carithers
    Brazilian Blue 817 by BM, 202
    Fernwood Green 2145-50 by BM, 192
Anne Carson
    Brilliant White by BM, 94
Darryl Carter
    Lookout Point 1646 by BM, 46
Diane Chapman
    Tangerine Fusion 083 by BM, 192
Clodagh
    Midnight Navy 2067-10 by BM, 172
Birch Coffey
    Carbon Copy 2117-10 by BM, 146
    Pale Moon OC-108 by BM, 111
Eric Cohler
    Chinese Blue 90 by FB, 60
Christopher Coleman
    Cool Aqua 2056-40 by BM, 145
Faye Cone
    DKC-54 by DKC, 56
Colin Cowie
    Shelburne Buff HC-28 by BM, 107
Elissa Cullman
    Blue Wave 2065-50 by BM, 65
    Dalila 319 by BM, 180
    Sangria 2006-20 by BM, 133
    Silken Pine 2144-50 by BM, 16
Justine Cushing
    Decorator's White Int. Rm by BM, 36
Mark Cutler
    P11130 by FPE, 87
Antonio Da Motta
    DKC-17 by DKC, 16
Carl D'Aquino
    Potpourri Green 2029-50 by BM, 184
Roger De Cabrol
    Patriot Blue 2064-20 by BM, 62
Mick De Giulio
    Great Barrington Green HC-122 by BM, 91
Athalie Derse
    Antique White 2207 by PL, 95
Barry Dixon
    Fowler Pink 39 by FB, 20
    Picture Gallery Red 42 by FB, 20

Clare Donohue
    Wedgewood Gray HC-146 by BM, 86
    Woodlawn Blue HC-147 by BM, 86
T. Keller Donovan
    Borrowed Light 235 by FB, 111
    Brown Sugar 2112-20 by BM, 107
    Linen White 70 by BM, 71
    Summer Shower 2135-60 by BM, 74
Kay Douglass
    Seapearl OC-19 by BM, 108, 109
Christopher Drake
    Showtime 923 by BM, 67
Jamie Drake
    Aruba Blue 2048-30 by BM, 169
    White Satin 2067-70 by BM, 121
    Windmill Wings 2067-60 by BM, 64
Mary Douglas Drysdale
    Jamaican Aqua 2048-60 by BM, 120
    Yam 290B-7 by BR, 162
Peter Dunham
    Blue Angel 2058-70 by BM, 179
    Citrus Blast 2018-30 by BM, 170
    Mahogany 36 by FB, 159
    Mystical Grape 2071-30 by BM, 170
    Oyster Bay SS61 by RLP, 16
    Pagoda Red 5-15 by PL, 130
Arthur Dunnam
    Branchport Brown HC-72 by BM, 102
Ann Dupuy
    Pink Ground 202 by FB, 202
David Easton
    Blazer 212 by FB, 129
    Moorish Red HC55 by Papers & Paints Ltd., 25
Sharone Einhorn
    November Rain 2142-60 by BM, 54
Chad Eisner
    Flint 32-30 by PL, 84, 85
    Silver Birch 18-31 by PL, 96
    Solitary 19-29 by PL, 96
Beverly Ellsley
    Golden Honey 297 by BM, 87
Mark Epstein
    Deep River 1582 by BM, 164
William Eubanks
    Golden Straw 2152-50 by BM, 75
Waldo Fernandez
    Holiday Wreath 447 by BM, 110

Susan Ferrier
  Brainstorm Bronze 7033 by SW, 98
  Carrington Beige HC-93 by BM, 98
  Danville Tan HC-91 by BM, 46
  Light Blue 22 by FB, 52
Maureen Footer
  Old World 2011-40 by BM, 190
Michael Formica
  California Blue 2060-20 by BM, 95
Ken Fulk
  Adobe O8 by PPC, 47
  Agua Verte PPC-BL7 by PPC, 41
  Mink PPC-G13 by PPC, 41
Steven Gambrel
  Argent 1322 by PL, 71
  Horizon 1478 by BM, 43
  Sea Star 2123-30 by BM, 47
Jennifer Garrigues
  Cloud White 967 by BM, 187
  Folly Green 76 by FB, 72
  Honied White 7106 by SW, 48
  Mesquite 501 by BM, 40
  Parsley Tint 6998-1 by Porter Paints, 187
Richard Gluckman
  Bear Creek 1470 by BM, 50
  China White Int. Rm by BM, 37
Tori Golub
  DKC-62 by DKC, 140
Mariette Himes Gomez
  DKC-51 by DKC, 34
  Green Ground 206 by FB, 43
  Sage Tint 458 by BM, 104
  String 8 by FB, 43
Robert Goodwin
  Iron Mountain 2134-30 by BM, 68
Philip Gorrivan
  Razzle Dazzle 1348 by BM, 88
Susan Zises Green
  Leamon Sirrup DMV070 by Duron Mount
    Vernon Estate of Colours, 124
  Menagerie 63 by FB, 180
S. Russell Groves
  Moss Green 16-29 by PL, 202
Thomas Gunkelman
  Bleeker Beige HC-80 by BM, 124
Alexa Hampton
  Ivory White 925 by BM, 33
  Tucson Red 1300 by BM, 133

Amelia Handegan
  LP-16 by FPE, 57
Ralph Harvard
  Pelham Gray Light CW-819 by PL, 99
  Verditer Blue DRC078 NRH by SW, 60
Thad Hayes
  DKC-64 by DKC, 97
Patricia Healing
  Dutch Chocolate 6012 by FPE, 69
  French Lilac 1403 by BM, 202
Jarrett Hedborg
  Santa Monica Blue 776 by BM, 184
  Tangerine Dream 2012-30 by BM, 97
Patricia Hill
  DKC-11 by DKC, 138
William Hodgins
  Deck Enamel Black C-112-80 by BM, 27
  Deck Enamel Rich Brown 60 by BM, 27
Myra Hoefer
  Bone 15 by FB, 197
  California Poppy GH170 by RLP, 141
  Down Pipe 26 by FB, 55
  Horizon Gray 2141-50 by BM, 81
  Misty Memories 2118-60 by BM, 190, 191
  Queen Anne Pink HC-60 by BM, 188
Phoebe Howard
  Blue Hubbard 8438 by SW, 65
  Clunch 2009 by FB, 18, 19
  Shaded White 201 by FB, 51
  Soft Pumpkin 2166-40 by BM, 172
Angie Hranowsky
  Jack Horner's Plum 1-20 by PL, 198, 199
  Persian Pink 6650-1 by Porter Paints, 178
  White Chocolate OC-127 by BM, 163
Joanne Hudson
  Whole Wheat SW6121 by SW, 87
Brooke Huttig
  Shagreen SW6422 by SW, 197
Kathryn M. Ireland
  Borrowed Light 235 by FB, 20
  Citron 74 by FB, 114
  Goldfinch GH105 by RLP, 180
Keith Irvine
  Coral Gables 2010-40 by BM, 173
  Dark Royal Blue 2065-20 by BM, 23
  Decorator's White Int. Rm by BM, 32, 33
  Linen White Int. Rm by BM, 32, 33
  Salsa 2009-20 by BM, 69
  Utah Sky 2065-40 by BM, 20

Thomas Jayne
    Acadia White OC-38 by BM, 34
    Blue Belle 782 by BM, 142, 143
    Camel Back 1103 by BM, 170
    Heavenly Blue 709 by BM, 62
    Scarecrow 1041 by BM, 88, 89
    Smashing Pink 1303 by BM, 142, 143
    Super White Int. Rm by BM, 142
Jay Jeffers
    Buxton Blue HC-149 by BM, 144
    Rust 2175-30 by BM, 144
Noel Jeffrey
    Morning Glory 785 by BM, 21
David Jimenez
    Starry Night Blue 2067-20 by BM, 58, 59
Kerry Joyce
    Studio Mauve 0062 by SW, 75
Suzanne Kasler
    Checkerberry 32RR50/260 by GL, 132
    Dressage Red TH41 by RLP, 129
    Elephant Tusk OC-8 by BM, 70
    Limoges Blue 30BG56/045 by GL, 115
    Orangery 70 by FB, 145
Cheryl Katz
    Coastal Fog AC-1 by BM, 18
Celerie Kemble
    Mere Green 219 by FB, 104
    31by Rollinson Hues, 186
Ellen Kennon
    Buttercream by FSP, 55
    Mushroom by FSP, 45
Philip Kirk
    Plantation White WN-18 by BR, 35
David Kleinberg
    Colony Green 694 by BM, 64
Todd Klein
    Man on the Moon OC-106 by BM, 21
Malcolm Kutner
    DKC-28 by DKC, 197
Amanda Kyser
    Deep Taupe 2111-10 by BM, 122, 123
    Merlot Red 2006-10 by BM, 90, 126, 127
    Onyx 2133-10 by BM, 78
    Valley Forge Brown HC-74 by BM, 136, 137
Jackye Lanham
    Magnetic Gray SW-7058 by SW, 192
Larry Laslo
    Ladybug Red 1322 by BM, 146
Amy Lau
    Rumba Orange 2014-20 by BM, 203

Martyn Lawrence-Bullard
    Blue Ground 210 by FB, 195
    Minster Green 224 by FB, 176, 177
    Orange Parrot 2169-20 by BM, 105
    Radicchio 96 by FB, 169
Sally Sirkin Lewis
    Smokey Taupe 983 by BM, 28
Suzanne Lovell
    DKC-66 by DKC, 21
Molly Luetkemeyer
    After the Storm DE5769 by DE, 156
Jodi Macklin
    DKC-20 by DKC, 164, 165
Hermes Mallea
    DKC-17 by DKC, 75
Carey Maloney
    DKC-10 by DKC, 152
David Mann
    Architectural Cream UL 55 by RLP, 95
Mallory Marshall
    Determined Orange 6635 by SW, 52
    Wenge AF-180 by BM, 44
Christopher Maya
    Blueberry Myrtille 1208-3 by PL, 154
    Glass Slipper 1632 by BM, 40
    Rectory Red 217 by FB, 140
Bobby McAlpine
    Linen UL03 by RLP, 160
    Walton Cream VM65 by RLP, 160
Gary McBournie
    Davenport Tan HC-76 by BM, 197
    Florida Pink 1320 by BM, 182, 183
    Red Parrot 1308 by BM, 57
    White Dove by BM, 182
Brian McCarthy
    Cayman Blue 2060-50 by BM, 112
    Oyster White by OFM, 153
    Slate by OFM, 153
Josie McCarthy
    Ivoire SW6127 by SW, 195
Mary McDonald
    Coconut Skin DE1055 by DE, 43
    Coral Pink 2003-50 by BM, 161
    Lavender Ice 2069-60 by BM, 82
    Romantic Pink 2004-70 by BM, 47
    Yellowhammer GH100 by RLP, 168
Ann McGuire
    Spring Squash 2008-1B by Valspar, 91
Mimi McMakin
    In the Pink SW 6583 by SW, 189

Lee Melahn
  Persian Violet 1419 by BM, 187
Richard Mishaan
  Chili Pepper 2004-20 by BM, 165
David Mitchell
  Sweet Dreams 847 by BM, 122
Charlotte Moss
  Blanched Coral 886 by BM, 113
  Breakfast Room Green 81 by FB, 102
  Vert de Terre 234 by FB, 27
Murray Moss
  Super White Int. Rm by BM, 34
David Netto
  Sun-Kissed Yellow 2022-20 by BM, 112
Jerome Neuner
  Super White Int. Rm by BM, 32
Philip Nimmo
  North Creek Brown 1001 by BM, 166, 167
Eugenie Niven
  Seafoam Green 2039-60 by BM, 192
Sandra Nunnerley
  Wolf Gray 2127-40 by BM, 91
Joe Nye
  Paprika 013 by Portola Paints, 130
  Shenandoah Taupe AC-36 by BM, 79
John Oetgen
  Palladian Blue HC-144 by BM, 69
Emily O'Keefe
  Master Room VM99 by RLP, 100, 101
Alex Papachristidis
  Opal Essence 680 by BM, 181
Peter Pennoyer
  Strong White 2001 by FB, 32
Paula Perlini
  Moroccan Red 1309 by BM, 171
  Riviera Azure 822 by BM, 118, 119
  Warm Sienna 1203 by BM, 87
Thomas Pheasant
  Ivory White 925 by BM, 37
Miles Redd
  Bird's Egg 2051-60 by BM, 114
  Colonial Rose 7102T by FPE, 170
  Heritage Red Ext. Rm by BM, 145
  Icy Blue 2057-70 by BM, 145
Suzanne Rheinstein
  Blue-Green GH81 by RLP, 179
  Crested Butte NA40 by RLP, 112
Katie Ridder
  Blazer 212 by FB, 156

Christopher Ridolfi
  Cooking Apple Green 32 by FB, 52
  Grant Beige HC-83 by BM, 43
Michael Roberson
  Powell Buff HC-35 by BM, 139
Markham Roberts
  Ivory White 925 by BM, 61
  Waterside 7573M by Parker Paint, 61
Eve Robinson
  Drab 41 by FB, 69
Todd Romano
  Blazer 212 by FB, 138
Frank Roop
  Expedition 162 by C2, 165
  Soft Fern 2144-40 by BM, 189
Jaime Rummerfield
  Hazel 6471 by SW, 150, 151
  Leapfrog 6341 by SW, 83
John Saladino
  Market Square Tavern Dark Green CW401 by
    Martin Senour, 140
  Oriental Iris 1418 by BM, 24
Franklin Salasky
  Mustang 2111-30 by BM, 139
Barbara Sallick
  Silver Satin OC-26 by BM, 97
Scott Sanders
  Coral Reef 012 by BM, 18
Fern Santini
  Nantucket Gray HC-111 by BM, 135
Tom Scheerer
  Deep Jungle 21-17 by PL, 57
Craig Schumacher
  Plantation White WN-18 by BR, 35
Roderick Shade
  Million Dollar Red 2003-10 by BM, 133
  Pink Corsage 1349 by BM, 162
Tom Sheerer
  Atrium White Int. Rm by BM, 106
  Chocolate Candy Brown 2107-10 by BM, 106
  Morning Sunshine 2018-50 by BM, 76, 77
Betty Sherrill
  Minster Green 224 by FB, 27
Stephen Shubel
  Cactus Café KM3431-3 by Kelly-Moore, 160
Stephen Sills
  Stone Harbor 2111-50 by BM, 55
Kathy Smith
  Biscuit 38 by FB, 44, 45
  Pale Earth 8133 by SW, 53

Michael Smith
  Coos Bay 19-31 by PL, 92, 93
  Silver Blond 14-29 by PL, 42
Matthew Patrick Smyth
  Linen White 70 by BM, 40
  Vintage Claret 1013 by PL, 124
  Wickham Gray HC-171 by BM, 57
Ruthie Sommers
  Blue Seafoam 2056-60 by BM, 62, 63
  Dutchlac Brilliant Tulip Red W1001B-M by
    FPE, 129
  Iceberg 2122-50 by BM, 54
  Relay Red IB11 by RLP, 153
  Sea Foam 2123-60 by BM, 184, 185
Alison Spear
  Ruby Red 2001-10 by BM, 128
Whitney Stewart
  Café Latte 7314 by C2, 147
  Chai 7293 by C2, 147
  Electric 275 by C2, 60
  Enoki 425 by C2, 163
  Quahog 8385 by C2, 72
Robert Stilin
  Cooking Apple Green 32 by FB, 120
Stephanie Stokes
  Claydon Blue 87 by FB, 136
  Fresh Dew 435 by BM, 99
Madeline Stuart
  Light Blue 22 by FB, 17
  Pale Hound 71 by FB, 49
James Swan
  Pearl White 29-29 by PL, 200, 201
  Rosa Lee 1-13 by PL, 200, 201
Rose Tarlow
  All White 2005 by FB, 24
  Pointing 2003 by FB, 24, 25
  Slipper Satin 2004 by FB, 24
Jackie Terrell
  Gloaming 2145 by PL, 195
  Lemon Freeze 2025-50 by BM, 186
  Nasturtium 1830 by PL, 195
Priscilla Ulmann
  Yellow Ground 218 by FB, 99
Erinn Valencich
  Deep Carnation DE5011 by DE, 165
Carleton Varney
  Little Angel 318 by BM, 152
  Super White Int. Rm by BM, 152

Peter Vaughn
  Mauve Bauhaus 1407 by BM, 125
  Spring Iris 1402 by BM, 125
Diana Vreeland
  Red 2000-10 by BM, 130, 131
Marshall Watson
  Chic Lime 396 by BM, 186
  DKC-37 by DKC, 114
  Humble Gold SW6380 by SW, 136
Kelly Wearstler
  Scarlet O'Hara 1870 by PL, 148
  Seed Pearl 27-32 by PL, 37
Barbara Westbrook
  DKC-5 by DKC, 26
  Overcast OC-43 by BM, 141
  Whitall Brown HC-69 by BM, 141
Michael Whaley
  Cedar Grove 444 by BM, 200
  Garden Cucumber 644 by BM, 139
Timothy Whealon
  Basalt VM121 by RLP, 186
Kendall Wilkinson
  Jet Stream 814 by BM, 203
  Linen White 70 by BM, 203
Robert Willson
  Swiss Coffee OC-45 by BM, 157
  Winter White 2140-70 by BM, 157
Bret Witke
  Powder Sand 2151-70 by BM, 107
Vicente Wolf
  Graytint 1611 by BM, 50
  Patriotic White 2135-70 by BM, 28
Honey Wolters
  November Rain 2142-60 by BM, 54
Eldon Wong
  Classic Pooh Butterfly Flutter By DC2A-10-1 by
    BR Disney Home, 72, 73
  Redstone 2009-10 by BM, 128
Ron Woodson
  Hazel 6471 by SW, 150, 151
  Leapfrog 6341 by SW, 83
Jack Young
  Coral Spice 2170-40 by BM, 48
John Yunis
  Aquarius 788 by BM, 62
  Sunnyside Lane 7014T by FPE, 120

INDEX

31 By Rollinson Hues, 186, 258
2030-G70Y By FPE, 179, 258

Acadia White OC-38 by BM, 34, 231
Adobe O8 by PPC, 47, 247
After the Storm DE5769 by DE, 156, 260
Agua Verte PPC-BL7 by PPC, 41, 237
Alabaster OC-129 by BM, 233
Alligator Alley 441 by BM, 162, 219, 259
All White 2005 by FB, 24, 231
Antique White 2207 by PL, 95, 223, 232
Aquarius 788 by BM, 62, 212, 268
Architectural Cream UL 55 by RLP, 95, 223, 234
Argent 1322 by PL, 71, 209, 263
Aruba Blue 2048-30 by BM, 169, 219, 259
Atrium White Int. Rm by BM, 106, 216, 233
Autumn Crocus 1141 by PL, 95, 152, 223, 272
Avoine de Mer 17-26 by PL, 111, 227, 236

Babouche 223 by FB, 105, 155, 245
Bagel 6114 by SW, 172, 173, 229, 238
Basalt VM121 by RLP, 186, 256
Bear Creek 1470 by BM, 50, 265
Behr (BR)
    Candy Coated 120B-5, 250
    Disney Home, Classic Pooh Butterfly Flutter
        By DC2A-10-1, 72, 73, 209, 271
    Plantation White WN-18, 35, 226, 261
    Yam 290B-7, 162, 246
Bella Donna C2-316 W by C2, 38, 39, 114, 211,
    226, 228, 271
Benjamin Moore (BM)
    Acadia White OC-38, 34, 231
    Alabaster OC-129, 233
    Alligator Alley 441, 162, 219, 259
    Aquarius 788, 62, 212, 268
    Aruba Blue 2048-30, 169, 219, 259
    Atrium White Int. Rm, 106, 216, 233
    Bear Creek 1470, 50, 265
    Bird's Egg 2051-60, 114, 229, 268
    Blanched Coral 886, 113, 228, 248
    Bleeker Beige HC-80, 124, 235
    Blue Angel 2058-70, 179, 267
    Blue Belle 782, 142, 143, 269
    Blue Seafoam 2056-60, 62, 63, 208, 264
    Blue Wave 2065-50, 65, 227, 268
    Branchport Brown HC-72, 102, 215, 241
    Brazilian Blue 817, 202, 272
    Brilliant White, 94, 223, 232
    Brown Sugar 2112-20, 107, 216, 242
    Buxton Blue HC-149, 144, 264
    California Blue 2060-20, 95, 223, 270

Calypso Orange 2015-30, 246
Camel Back 1103, 170, 239
Carbon Copy 2117-10, 146, 270
Carrington Beige HC-93, 98, 224, 240
Cayman Blue 2060-50, 112, 228, 268
Cedar Grove 444, 200, 264
Chic Lime 396, 186, 257
Chili Pepper 2004-20, 165, 229, 253
China White Int. Rm, 37, 232
Chocolate Candy Brown 2107-10, 106, 216,
    242
Citrus Blast 2018-30, 170, 246
Clearest Ocean Blue 2064-40, 269
Coastal Fog AC-1, 18, 211, 235
Colony Green 694, 64, 227, 263
Cool Aqua 2056-40, 145, 268
Coral Gables 2010-40, 173, 219, 250
Coral Pink 2003-50, 161, 250
Coral Reef 012, 18, 226, 250
Coral Spice 2170-40, 48, 211, 251
Dalila 319, 180, 244
Danville Tan HC-91, 46, 239
Dark Royal Blue 2065-20, 23, 214, 270
Davenport Tan HC-76, 197, 241
Deck Enamel Black C-112-80, 27, 266
Deck Enamel Rich Brown 60, 27, 241
Decorator's White Int. Rm, 32, 33, 36, 231
Deep River 1582, 164, 260
Deep Taupe 2111-10, 122, 123, 218, 242
Elephant Tusk OC-8, 70, 209, 262
Essex Green Ext. Rm, 155, 260
Fernwood Green 2145-50, 192, 257
Festive Orange 2014-10, 205, 247
Florida Pink 1320, 182, 183, 225, 251
French Lilac 1403, 202, 214, 272
Fresh Dew 435, 99, 224, 256
Garden Cucumber 644, 139, 260
Gentle Violet 2071-20, 207, 273
Glass Slipper 1632, 40, 218, 267
Golden Honey 297, 87, 220, 244
Golden Straw 2152-50, 75, 210, 244
Grant Beige HC-83, 43, 235
Grappa 1393, 160, 273
Graytint 1611, 50, 208, 265
Great Barrington Green HC-122, 91, 169, 219,
    221, 259
Heavenly Blue 709, 62, 263
Hepplewhite Ivory HC-36, 102, 103, 215, 237
Heritage Red Ext. Rm, 145, 154, 155, 253
Holiday Wreath 447, 110, 227, 265
Horizon 1478, 43, 234
Horizon Gray 2141-50, 81, 212, 262

Iceberg 2122-50, 54, 211, 264
Icy Blue 2057-70, 145, 266
Iron Mountain 2134-30, 68, 208, 266
Ivory White 925, 33, 37, 61, 231
Jamaican Aqua 2048-60, 120, 267
Jet Stream 814, 203, 230, 272
Ladybug Red 1322, 80, 146, 212, 253
Lavender Ice 2069-60, 82, 212, 237
Lemon Freeze 2025-50, 186, 257
Linen White Int. Rm, 32, 33
Linen White 70, 40, 71, 203, 209, 233
Little Angel 318, 152, 244
Lookout Point 1646, 46, 267
Madison Avenue 759, 229, 259
Man on the Moon OC-106, 21, 211, 232
Mauve Bauhaus 1407, 125
Merlot Red 2006-10, 90, 126, 127, 129, 218, 221, 254
Mesquite 501, 40, 261
Midnight Navy 2067-10, 172, 230, 270
Milano Red 1313, 120, 121, 249
Million Dollar Red 2003-10, 133, 254
Misty Lilac 2071-70, 111, 227, 271
Misty Memories 2118-60, 190, 191, 264
Morning Glory 785, 21, 226, 268
Morning Sunshine 2018-50, 76, 77, 212, 237
Moroccan Red 1309, 171, 217, 253
Mustang 2111-30, 139, 229, 241
Mystical Grape 2071-30, 170, 273
Nantucket Gray HC-111, 135, 262
Narragansett Green HC-157, 15, 208
North Creek Brown 1001, 166, 167, 241
November Rain 2142-60, 54, 262
Old World 2011-40, 190, 250
Onyx 2133-10, 78, 212, 241
Opal Essence 680, 181, 230, 256
Orange Parrot 2169-20, 105, 215, 247
Oriental Iris 1418, 24, 272
Overcast OC-43, 141
Paddington Blue 791, 64, 269
Pale Moon OC-108, 111, 227, 244
Pale Vista 2029-60, 45, 256
Palladian Blue HC-144, 69, 209, 263
Papaya 957, 45, 238
Patriot Blue 2064-20, 62, 218, 270
Patriotic White 2135-70, 28, 266
Peace and Happiness 1380, 46, 271
Peony 2079-30, 200, 225, 249
Persian Violet 1419, 187, 272
Pink Corsage 1349, 162, 222, 249
Potpourri Green 2029-50, 184, 257
Powder Sand 2151-70, 107, 216, 233

Powell Buff HC-35, 139, 213, 236
Queen Anne Pink HC-60, 188, 230, 234
Raccoon Hollow 978, 48, 261
Razzle Dazzle 1348, 88, 221, 249
Red 2000-10, 130, 131, 229, 252
Red Parrot 1308, 57, 222, 250
Redstone 2009-10, 128, 216, 253
Riviera Azure 822, 118, 119, 229, 272
Romantic Pink 2004-70, 47, 248
Ruby Red 2001-10, 128, 213, 252
Rumba Orange 2014-20, 203, 247
Rust 2175-30, 144, 255
Saddle Soap 2110-30, 80, 212, 241
Sage Tint 458, 104, 216, 263
Salsa 2009-20, 69, 208, 253
Sangria 2006-20, 133, 254
Santa Monica Blue 776, 184, 269
Scarecrow 1041, 88, 89, 221, 240
Sea Foam 2123-60, 184, 185, 259
Seafoam Green 2039-60, 192
Seapearl OC-19, 108, 109, 227, 239
Sea Star 2123-30, 47, 264
Shelburne Buff HC-28, 107, 216, 238
Shenandoah Taupe AC-36, 79, 212, 241
Showtime 923, 67, 208, 245
Silken Pine 2144-50, 16, 226, 234
Silver Satin OC-26, 97, 224, 232
Smashing Pink 1303, 142, 143, 206, 248
Smoke Embers 1466, 193, 213, 262
Smokey Taupe 983, 28, 235
Soft Fern 2144-40, 189, 261
Soft Pumpkin 2166-40, 172, 246
Spring Iris 1402, 125, 271
Starry Night Blue 2067-20, 58, 59, 226, 270
Stone Harbor 2111-50, 55, 262
Stonington Gray HC-170, 15, 266
Straw 2154-50, 200, 214, 236
Summer Blue 2067-50, 147, 272
Summer Shower 2135-60, 74, 210, 267
Sundance 2022-50, 28, 211, 214, 244
Sun-Kissed Yellow 2022-20, 112, 228, 245
Super White Int. Rm, 32, 34, 142, 152, 231
Sweet Dreams 847, 122, 256
Sweet Taffy 2086-60, 207, 248
Swiss Coffee OC-45, 157, 233
Tangerine Dream 2012-30, 97, 224, 247
Tangerine Fusion 083, 192, 247
Tucson Red 1300, 133, 217, 254
Tudor Brown, 80, 212, 243
Utah Sky 2065-40, 20, 208, 269
Valley Forge Brown HC-74, 136, 137, 229, 239
Van Buren Brown HC-70, 48, 194, 230, 242

Warm Sienna 1203, 87, 220, 252
Wedgewood Gray HC-146, 86, 220, 263
Wenge AF-180, 44, 242
Whitall Brown HC-69, 141, 240
White Chocolate OC-127, 163, 234
White Dove, 66, 74, 89, 182
White Satin 2067-70, 121, 267
Wickham Gray HC-171, 57
Windham Cream HC-6, 156, 236
Windmill Wings 2067-60, 64, 271
Winter White 2140-70, 157, 232
Wispy Green 414, 104, 215, 256
Wolf Gray 2127-40, 91, 221, 265
Woodlawn Blue HC-147, 86, 220, 263
Bird's Egg 2051-60 by BM, 114, 229, 268
Biscuit 38 by FB, 44, 45, 211, 239
Blanched Coral 886 by BM, 113, 228, 248
Blazer 212 by FB, 129, 138, 156, 252
Bleeker Beige HC-80 by BM, 124, 235
Blue Angel 2058-70 by BM, 179, 267
Blue Belle 782 by BM, 142, 143, 269
Blueberry Myrtille 1208-3 by PL, 154, 270
Blue Cart 094 by Portola Paints, 269
Blue-Green GH81 by RLP, 179, 264
Blue Ground 210 by FB, 180, 195, 268
Blue Hubbard 8438 by SW, 65, 227, 266
Blue Seafoam 2056-60 by BM, 62, 63, 208, 264
Blue Wave 2065-50 by BM, 65, 227, 268
BM. See Benjamin Moore (BM)
Bone 15 by FB, 197, 235
Borrowed Light 235 by FB, 20, 111, 226, 227, 267
BR. See Behr (BR)
Brady, Stephen, Bagel 6114 by SW, 172, 173
Brainstorm Bronze 7033 by SW, 98, 224, 243
Branchport Brown HC-72 by BM, 102, 215, 241
Brazilian Blue 817 by BM, 202, 272
Breakfast Room Green 81 by FB, 102, 215, 258
Brilliant White by BM, 94, 223, 232
Brown Sugar 2112-20 by BM, 107, 216, 242
Buttercream by FSP, 55, 236
Butterfly Flutter By DC2A-10-1 by BR Disney
   Home, 73
Buxton Blue HC-149 by BM, 144, 264

C2
   Bella Donna C2-316 W, 38, 39, 114, 211, 226,
      228, 271
   Café Latte 7314, 147, 238
   Chai 7293, 147, 237
   Electric 275, 60, 270
   Enoki 425, 163, 213, 237
   Expedition 162, 165, 210, 259

Quahog 8385, 72, 210, 239
Salty Brine C2-4388, 258
Sorcerer 5326, 52, 215, 270
Cactus Café KM3431-3 by Kelly-Moore, 160, 258
Café Latte 7314 by C2, 147, 238
California Blue 2060-20 by BM, 95, 223, 270
California Poppy GH170 by RLP, 141, 213, 247
Calypso Orange 2015-30 by BM, 246
Calypso VM138 by RLP, 104, 216, 273
Camel Back 1103 by BM, 170, 239
Canary Yellow 12-8 by PL, 204, 245
Candy Coated 120B-5 by BR, 250
Carbon Copy 2117-10 by BM, 146, 270
Carrington Beige HC-93 by BM, 98, 224, 240
Cayman Blue 2060-50 by BM, 112, 228, 268
Cedar Grove 444 by BM, 200, 264
Chai 7293 by C2, 147, 237
Checkerberry 32RR50/260 by GL, 132, 217, 248
Chic Lime 396 by BM, 186, 257
Chili Pepper 2004-20 by BM, 165, 229, 253
China White Int. Rm by BM, 37, 232
Chinese Blue 90 by FB, 60, 269
Chocolate Candy Brown 2107-10 by BM, 106, 216,
   242
Ciara Yellow 73 by FB, 245
Citron 74 by FB, 114, 228, 245
Citrus Blast 2018-30 by BM, 170, 246
Classic Pooh Butterfly Flutter by DC2A-10-1 by BR
   Disney Home, 72, 73, 209, 271
Claydon Blue 87 by FB, 136, 218, 265
Clearest Ocean Blue 2064-40 by BM, 269
Clunch 2009 by FB, 18, 19, 218, 238
Coastal Fog AC-1 by BM, 18, 211, 235
Coconut Skin DE1055 by DE, 43, 241
Colonial Rose 7102T by FPE, 170, 229, 250
Colony Green 694 by BM, 64, 227, 263
Cooking Apple Green 32 by FB, 52, 120, 211, 218,
   258
Cool Aqua 2056-40 by BM, 145, 268
Coos Bay 19-31 by PL, 92, 93, 223, 264
Coral Gables 2010-40 by BM, 173, 219, 250
Coral Pink 2003-50 by BM, 161, 250
Coral Reef 012 by BM, 18, 226, 250
Coral Spice 2170-40 by BM, 48, 211, 251
Cream Stone UL54 by RLP, 88, 221, 237
Crested Butte NA40 by RLP, 112, 228, 239

Dalila 319 by BM, 180, 244
Danville Tan HC-91 by BM, 46, 239
Dark Royal Blue 2065-20 by BM, 23, 214, 270
Davenport Tan HC-76 by BM, 197, 241
DE. See Dunn-Edwards (DE)

Deck Enamel Black C-112-80 by BM, 27, 266
Deck Enamel Rich Brown 60 by BM, 27, 241
Decorator's White Int. Rm by BM, 32, 33, 36, 231
Deep Carnation DE5011 by DE, 165, 217, 273
Deep Jungle 21-17 by PL, 57, 260
Deep River 1582 by BM, 164, 260
Deep Taupe 2111-10 by BM, 122, 123, 218, 242
Desert Boot TH35 by RLP, 107, 216, 242
Desert Orange 78YR39/593 by GL, 204, 246
Determined Orange 6635 by SW, 52, 247
Dimity 2008 by FB, 97, 223, 248
DKC. See Donald Kaufman Color Collection
  (DKC)
Donald Kaufman Color Collection (DKC)
    DKC-5, 26, 232
    DKC-8, 51, 261
    DKC-10, 152, 261
    DKC-11, 138, 257
    DKC-17, 16, 75, 208, 210, 254
    DKC-20, 50, 164, 165, 245
    DKC-23, 146, 222, 258
    DKC-28, 197, 233
    DKC-30, 122, 244
    DKC-37, 114, 228, 267
    DKC-51, 34, 231
    DKC-54, 56, 234
    DKC-62, 140, 261
    DKC-64, 97, 224, 239
    DKC-66, 21, 218, 242
Down Pipe 26 by FB, 55, 220, 265
Drab 41 by FB, 69, 209, 239
Dressage Red TH41 by RLP, 129, 254
Drum Beat 00YR08/409 by GL, 204, 255
Dunn-Edwards (DE)
    After the Storm DE5769, 156, 260
    Coconut Skin DE1055, 43, 241
    Deep Carnation DE5011, 165, 217, 273
    Perfect Pear DE5519, 195, 256
Duron Mount Vernon Estate of Colours, Leamon
  Sirrup DMV070, 124, 256
Dutch Chocolate 6012 by FPE, 69, 209, 243
Dutchlac Brilliant Tulip Red W1001B-M by FPE,
  129, 225, 252

Electric 275 by C2, 60, 270
Elephant Tusk OC-8 by BM, 70, 209, 262
Enoki 425 by C2, 163, 213, 237
Essex Green Ext. Rm by BM, 155, 260
Expedition 162 by C2, 165, 210, 259

Farrow & Ball (FB)
    All White 2005, 24, 231
    Babouche 223, 105, 155, 245
    Biscuit 38, 44, 45, 211, 239
    Blazer 212, 129, 138, 156, 252
    Blue Ground 210, 180, 195, 268
    Bone 15, 197, 235
    Borrowed Light 235, 20, 111, 226, 227, 267
    Breakfast Room Green 81, 102, 215, 258
    Chinese Blue 90, 60, 269
    Ciara Yellow 73, 245
    Citron 74, 114, 228, 245
    Claydon Blue 87, 136, 218, 265
    Clunch 2009, 18, 19, 218, 238
    Cooking Apple Green 32, 52, 120, 211, 218,
      258
    Dimity 2008, 97, 223, 248
    Down Pipe 26, 55, 220, 265
    Drab 41, 69, 209, 239
    Folly Green 76, 72, 209, 258
    Fowler Pink 39, 20, 250
    Green Blue 84, 112, 228, 263
    Green Ground 206, 43, 257
    Light Blue 22, 17, 52, 208, 222, 262
    Mahogany 36, 159, 242
    Matchstick 2013, 29, 226, 233
    Menagerie 63, 180, 251
    Mere Green 219, 104, 215, 259
    Minster Green 224, 27, 176, 177, 218, 260
    Orangery 70, 145, 217, 246
    Pale Hound 71, 49, 226, 236
    Picture Gallery Red 42, 20, 254
    Pink Ground 202, 202, 248
    Pointing 2003, 24, 25, 105, 232
    Radicchio 96, 169, 219
    Rectory Red 217, 140, 253
    Shaded White 201, 51, 214, 261
    Slipper Satin 2004, 24, 234
    String 8, 43, 238
    Strong White 2001, 32, 232
    Tallow 203, 233
    Vert de Terre 234, 27, 261
    Yellow Ground 218, 99, 224, 245
FB. See Farrow & Ball (FB)
Fernwood Green 2145-50 by BM, 192, 257
Festive Orange 2014-10 by BM, 205, 247
Fine Paints of Europe (FPE)
    Colonial Rose 7102T, 170, 229, 250
    Dutch Chocolate 6012, 69, 209, 243
    Dutchlac Brilliant Tulip Red W1001B-M, 129,
      225, 252
    LP-16, 57, 237

P11130, 87, 220, 257
Spinnaker White 7032, 75, 210, 231
Sunnyside Lane 7014T, 120, 244
2030-G70Y, 179, 258
Wintersweet Berry 5104T, 251
Flint 32-30 by PL, 84, 85, 220, 240
Florida Pink 1320 by BM, 182, 183, 225, 251
Folly Green 76 by FB, 72, 209, 258
Forward Fuschia SW 6842 by SW, 207, 249
Fowler Pink 39 by FB, 20, 250
FPE. See Fine Paints of Europe (FPE)
French Lilac 1403 by BM, 202, 214, 272
Fresh Cream 11-5 by PL, 181, 235
Fresh Dew 435 by BM, 99, 224, 256
FSP. See Full Spectrum Paints (FSP)
Full Spectrum Paints (FSP)
    Buttercream, 55, 236
    Mushroom, 45, 233

Garden Cucumber 644 by BM, 139, 260
Gentle Violet 2071-20 by BM, 207, 273
Geranium 005 by Portola Paints, 249
GL. See Glidden (GL)
Glass Slipper 1632 by BM, 40, 218, 267
Glidden (GL)
    Checkerberry 32RR50/260, 132, 217, 248
    Desert Orange 78YR39/593, 204, 246
    Drum Beat 00YR08/409, 204, 255
    Icon Grey 1677, 265
    Limoges Blue 30BG56/045, 115, 228, 271
    Peachglow 90YR71/144, 206, 248
    Vesper 70RB67/067, 206, 249
    Yellow Gold 758, 245
Gloaming 2145 by PL, 195, 240
Golden Honey 297 by BM, 87, 220, 244
Golden Straw 2152-50 by BM, 75, 210, 244
Goldfinch GH105 by RLP, 180, 244
Grant Beige HC-83 by BM, 43, 235
Grappa 1393 by BM, 160, 273
Graytint 1611 by BM, 50, 208, 265
Great Barrington Green HC-122 by BM, 91, 169, 219, 221, 259
Green Blue 84 by FB, 112, 228, 263
Green Ground 206 by FB, 43, 257
Gunnel 25-23 by PL, 196, 265
Gusto Gold SW 6904 by SW, 205, 246

Hazel 6471 by SW, 150, 151, 210, 263
Heavenly Blue 709 by BM, 62, 263
Hepplewhite Ivory HC-36 by BM, 102, 103, 215, 237
Heritage Red Ext. Rm by BM, 145, 154, 155, 253

Holiday Wreath 447 by BM, 110, 227, 265
Honied White 7106 by SW, 48, 235
Horizon 1478 by BM, 43, 234
Horizon Gray 2141-50 by BM, 81, 212, 262
Humble Gold SW6380 by SW, 136, 236

Iceberg 2122-50 by BM, 54, 211, 264
Icon Grey 1677 by GL, 265
Icy Blue 2057-70 by BM, 145, 266
In the Pink SW 6583 by SW, 189, 250
Iron Mountain 2134-30 by BM, 68, 208, 266
Ivoire SW6127 by SW, 195, 236
Ivory White 925 by BM, 33, 37, 61, 231

Jack Horner's Plum 1-20 by PL, 198, 199, 217, 273
Jamaican Aqua 2048-60 by BM, 120, 267
Jet Stream 814 by BM, 203, 230, 272

Kelly-Moore, Cactus Café KM3431-3, 160, 258

Ladybug Red 1322 by BM, 80, 146, 212, 253
Lattice Red 1B57 by RLP, 133, 252
Lavender Ice 2069-60 by BM, 82, 212, 237
Leamon Sirrup DMV070 by Duron Mount Vernon
    Estate of Colours, 124, 256
Leapfrog 6341 by SW, 83, 213, 259
Lemon Freeze 2025-50 by BM, 186, 257
Lifevest Orange IB64 by RLP, 205, 252
Light Blue 22 by FB, 17, 52, 208, 222, 262
Limoges Blue 30BG56/045 by GL, 115, 228, 271
Linen UL03 by RLP, 160, 262
Linen White Int. Rm by BM, 32, 33
Linen White 70 by BM, 40, 71, 203, 209, 233
Little Angel 318 by BM, 152, 244
Lookout Point 1646 by BM, 46, 267
LP-16 by FPE, 57, 237

Madison Avenue 759 by BM, 229, 259
Magnetic Gray SW-7058 by SW, 192, 262
Mahogany 36 by FB, 159, 242
Mai Tai IB58 by RLP, 205, 252
Man on the Moon OC-106 by BM, 21, 211, 232
Market Square Tavern Dark Green CW401 by
    Martin Senour, 140, 219, 260
Martin Senour, Market Square Tavern Dark Green
    CW401, 140, 219, 260
Master Room VM99 by RLP, 100, 101, 215, 240
Matchstick 2013 by FB, 29, 226, 233
Mauve Bauhaus 1407 by BM, 125
Menagerie 63 by FB, 180, 251
Mere Green 219 by FB, 104, 215, 259

Merlot Red 2006-10 by BM, 90, 126, 127, 129, 218, 221, 254
Mesquite 501 by BM, 40, 261
Midnight Navy 2067-10 by BM, 172, 230, 270
Milano Red 1313 by BM, 120, 121, 249
Million Dollar Red 2003-10 by BM, 133, 254
Mink PPC-G13 by PPC, 41, 240
Minster Green 224 by FB, 27, 176, 177, 218, 260
Misty Lilac 2071-70 by BM, 111, 227, 271
Misty Memories 2118-60 by BM, 190, 191, 264
Modern Masters, Venetian Blue ME-429, 148, 269
Moorish Red HC55 by Papers & Paints Ltd., 25, 251
Morning Glory 785 by BM, 21, 226, 268
Morning Sunshine 2018-50 by BM, 76, 77, 212, 237
Moroccan Red 1309 by BM, 171, 217, 253
Moss Green 16-29 by PL, 202, 257
Mushroom by FSP, 45, 233
Mustang 2111-30 by BM, 139, 229, 241
Mystical Grape 2071-30 by BM, 170, 273

Nantucket Gray HC-111 by BM, 135, 262
Narragansett Green HC-157 by BM, 15, 208
Nasturtium 1830 by PL, 195, 247
North Creek Brown 1001 by BM, 166, 167, 241
November Rain 2142-60 by BM, 54, 262

OFM. See Old Fashioned Milk Paint Co. (OFM)
Old Fashioned Milk Paint Co. (OFM)
    Oyster White, 153, 234
    Slate, 153, 265
Old World 2011-40 by BM, 190, 250
Onyx 2133-10 by BM, 78, 212, 241
Opal Essence 680 by BM, 181, 230, 256
Orange Parrot 2169-20 by BM, 105, 215, 247
Orangery 70 by FB, 145, 217, 246
Oriental Iris 1418 by BM, 24, 272
Oriental Night 29-14 by PL, 206, 273
Overcast OC-43 by BM, 141
Oyster Bay SS61 by RLP, 16, 259
Oyster White by OFM, 153, 234

P11130 by FPE, 87, 220, 257
Paddington Blue 791 by BM, 64, 269
Pagoda Red 5-15 by PL, 130, 225, 254
Pale Earth 8133 by SW, 53, 222, 237
Pale Hound 71 by FB, 49, 226, 236
Pale Moon OC-108 by BM, 111, 227, 244
Pale Vista 2029-60 by BM, 45, 256
Palladian Blue HC-144 by BM, 69, 209, 263
Papaya 957 by BM, 45, 238

Papers & Paints Ltd., Moorish Red HC55, 25, 251
Paprika 013 by Portola Paints, 130, 252
Parker Paint, Waterside 7573M, 61, 215, 268
Parsley Tint 6998-1 by Porter Paints, 187, 230, 256
Patriot Blue 2064-20 by BM, 62, 218, 270
Patriotic White 2135-70 by BM, 28, 266
Peace and Happiness 1380 by BM, 46, 271
Peachglow 90YR71/144 by GL, 206, 248
Pearl White 29-29 by PL, 200, 201, 235
Pearly Gates 2268 by PL, 193
Pelham Gray Light CW-819 by PL, 99, 224, 235
Peony 2079-30 by BM, 200, 225, 249
Perfect Pear DE5519 by DE, 195, 256
Peridot 18-20 by PL, 148, 149, 264
Persian Pink 6650-1 by Porter Paints, 178, 213, 249
Persian Violet 1419 by BM, 187, 272
Philip's Perfect Color (PPC)
    Adobe O8, 47, 247
    Agua Verte PPC-BL7, 41, 237
    Mink PPC-G13, 41, 240
Picture Gallery Red 42 by FB, 20, 254
Pink Corsage 1349 by BM, 162, 222, 249
Pink Ground 202 by FB, 202, 248
PL. See Pratt & Lambert (PL)
Plantation White WN-18 by BR, 35, 226, 261
Pocket Watch White WW11 by RLP, 37, 231
Pointing 2003 by FB, 24, 25, 105, 232
Porter Paints
    Parsley Tint 6998-1, 187, 230, 256
    Persian Pink 6650-1, 178, 213, 249
Portola Paints
    Blue Cart 094, 269
    Geranium 005, 249
    Paprika 013, 130, 252
Potpourri Green 2029-50 by BM, 184, 257
Powder Sand 2151-70 by BM, 107, 216, 233
Powell Buff HC-35 by BM, 139, 213, 236
PPC. See Philip's Perfect Color (PPC)
Pratt & Lambert (PL)
    Antique White 2207, 95, 223, 232
    Argent 1322, 71, 209, 263
    Autumn Crocus 1141, 95, 152, 223, 272
    Avoine de Mer 17-26, 111, 227, 236
    Blueberry Myrtille 1208-3, 154, 270
    Canary Yellow 12-8, 204, 245
    Coos Bay 19-31, 92, 93, 223, 264
    Deep Jungle 21-17, 57, 260
    Flint 32-30, 84, 85, 220, 240
    Fresh Cream 11-5, 181, 235
    Gloaming 2145, 195, 240
    Gunnel 25-23, 196, 265
    Jack Horner's Plum 1-20, 198, 199, 217, 273

Moss Green 16-29, 202, 257
Nasturtium 1830, 195, 247
Oriental Night 29-14, 206, 273
Pagoda Red 5-15, 130, 225, 254
Pearl White 29-29, 200, 201, 235
Pearly Gates 2268, 193
Pelham Gray Light CW-819, 99, 224, 235
Peridot 18-20, 148, 149, 264
Rosa Lee 1-13, 200, 201, 214, 273
Scarlet O'Hara 1870, 148, 253
Seed Pearl 27-32, 37, 231
Silver Birch 18-31, 96, 223, 240
Silver Blond 14-29, 42, 220, 238
Silver Lining 32-32, 31, 234
Solitary 19-29, 96, 223, 238
Tampico 1411, 91, 221, 258
Trooper 26-14, 207, 272
Tulipe Violet 30-14, 206, 273
Vintage Claret 1013, 124, 213, 253
Wendigo 2293, 99, 224, 242
Windsor Blue 27-19, 181, 269
Prussian Blue VM122 by RLP, 146, 267

Quahog 8385 by C2, 72, 210, 239
Queen Anne Pink HC-60 by BM, 188, 230, 234

Raccoon Hollow 978 by BM, 48, 261
Racer Pink 1B07 by RLP, 71, 209, 249
Radicchio 96 by FB, 169, 219
Ralph Lauren Paint (RLP)
    Architectural Cream UL 55, 95, 223, 234
    Basalt VM121, 186, 256
    Blue-Green GH81, 179, 264
    California Poppy GH170, 141, 213, 247
    Calypso VM138, 104, 216, 273
    Cream Stone UL54, 88, 221, 237
    Crested Butte NA40, 112, 228, 239
    Desert Boot TH35, 107, 216, 242
    Dressage Red TH41, 129, 254
    Goldfinch GH105, 180, 244
    Lattice Red 1B57, 133, 252
    Lifevest Orange IB64, 205, 252
    Linen UL03, 160, 262
    Mai Tai IB58, 205, 252
    Master Room VM99, 100, 101, 215, 240
    Oyster Bay SS61, 16, 259
    Pocket Watch White WW11, 37, 231
    Prussian Blue VM122, 146, 267
    Racer Pink 1B07, 71, 209, 249
    Relay Red IB11, 153, 254
    Walton Cream VM65, 160, 248

Weathered Brown UL44, 88, 221, 240
    Yellowhammer GH100, 168, 213, 236
Razzle Dazzle 1348 by BM, 88, 221, 249
Rectory Red 217 by FB, 140, 253
Red 2000-10 by BM, 130, 131, 229, 252
Red Parrot 1308 by BM, 57, 222, 250
Redstone 2009-10 by BM, 128, 216, 253
Relay Red IB11 by RLP, 153, 254
Riviera Azure 822 by BM, 118, 119, 229, 272
RLP. See Ralph Lauren Paint (RLP)
Rollinson Hues, 31, 186, 258
Romano, Todd, Blazer 212 by FB, 138
Romantic Pink 2004-70 by BM, 47, 248
Rosa Lee 1-13 by PL, 200, 201, 214, 273
Ruby Red 2001-10 by BM, 128, 213, 252
Rumba Orange 2014-20 by BM, 203, 247
Rust 2175-30 by BM, 144, 255

Saddle Soap 2110-30 by BM, 80, 212, 241
Sage Tint 458 by BM, 104, 216, 263
Salsa 2009-20 by BM, 69, 208, 253
Salty Brine C2-4388 by C2, 258
Sangria 2006-20 by BM, 133, 254
Santa Monica Blue 776 by BM, 184, 269
Sassy Blue 1241 by SW, 60, 271
Scarecrow 1041 by BM, 88, 89, 221, 240
Scarlet O'Hara 1870 by PL, 148, 253
Sea Foam 2123-60 by BM, 184, 185, 259
Seafoam Green 2039-60 by BM, 192
Seapearl OC-19 by BM, 108, 109, 227, 239
Sea Star 2123-30 by BM, 47, 264
Seed Pearl 27-32 by PL, 37, 231
Shaded White 201 by FB, 51, 214, 261
Shagreen SW6422 by SW, 197, 257
Shelburne Buff HC-28 by BM, 107, 216, 238
Shenandoah Taupe AC-36 by BM, 79, 212, 241
Sherwin-Williams (SW)
    Bagel 6114, 172, 173, 229, 238
    Blue Hubbard 8438, 65, 227, 266
    Brainstorm Bronze 7033, 98, 224, 243
    Determined Orange 6635, 52, 247
    Forward Fuschia SW 6842, 207, 249
    Gusto Gold SW 6904, 205, 246
    Hazel 6471, 150, 151, 210, 263
    Honied White 7106, 48, 235
    Humble Gold SW6380, 136, 236
    In the Pink SW 6583, 189, 250
    Ivoire SW6127, 195, 236
    Leapfrog 6341, 83, 213, 259
    Magnetic Gray SW-7058, 192, 262
    Pale Earth 8133, 53, 222, 237
    Sassy Blue 1241, 60, 271

Shagreen SW6422, 197, 257
Studio Mauve 0062, 75, 210, 271
Sunflower SW 6678, 246
Verditer Blue DRC078 NRH, 60, 211, 268
Whole Wheat SW6121, 87, 220, 238
Showtime 923 by BM, 67, 208, 245
Silken Pine 2144-50 by BM, 16, 226, 234
Silver Birch 18-31 by PL, 96, 223, 240
Silver Blond 14-29 by PL, 42, 220, 238
Silver Lining 32-32 by PL, 31, 234
Silver Satin OC-26 by BM, 97, 224, 232
Slate by OFM, 153, 265
Slipper Satin 2004 by FB, 24, 234
Smashing Pink 1303 by BM, 142, 143, 206, 248
Smoke Embers 1466 by BM, 193, 213, 262
Smokey Taupe 983 by BM, 28, 235
Soft Fern 2144-40 by BM, 189, 261
Soft Pumpkin 2166-40 by BM, 172, 246
Solitary 19-29 by PL, 96, 223, 238
Sorcerer 5326 by C2, 52, 215, 270
Spinnaker White 7032 by FPE, 75, 210, 231
Spring Iris 1402 by BM, 125, 271
Spring Squash 2008-1B by Valspar, 91, 221, 246
Starry Night Blue 2067-20 by BM, 58, 59, 226, 270
Stone Harbor 2111-50 by BM, 55, 262
Stonington Gray HC-170 by BM, 15, 266
Straw 2154-50 by BM, 200, 214, 236
String 8 by FB, 43, 238
Strong White 2001 by FB, 32, 232
Studio Mauve 0062 by SW, 75, 210, 271
Summer Blue 2067-50 by BM, 147, 272
Summer Shower 2135-60 by BM, 74, 210, 267
Sundance 2022-50 by BM, 28, 211, 214, 244
Sunflower SW 6678 by SW, 246
Sun-Kissed Yellow 2022-20 by BM, 112, 228, 245
Sunnyside Lane 7014T by FPE, 120, 244
Super White Int. Rm by BM, 32, 34, 142, 152, 231
SW. See Sherwin-Williams (SW)
Sweet Dreams 847 by BM, 122, 256
Sweet Taffy 2086-60 by BM, 207, 248
Swiss Coffee OC-45 by BM, 157, 233

Tallow 203 by FB, 233
Tampico 1411 by PL, 91, 221, 258
Tangerine Dream 2012-30 by BM, 97, 224, 247

Tangerine Fusion 083 by BM, 192, 247
Trooper 26-14 by PL, 207, 272
Tucson Red 1300 by BM, 133, 217, 254
Tudor Brown by BM, 80, 212, 243
Tulipe Violet 30-14 by PL, 206, 273

Utah Sky 2065-40 by BM, 20, 208, 269
Valley Forge Brown HC-74 by BM, 136, 137, 229, 239
Valspar, Spring Squash 2008-1B, 91, 221, 246
Van Buren Brown HC-70 by BM, 48, 194, 230, 242
Venetian Blue ME-429 by Modern Masters, 148, 269
Verditer Blue DRC078 NRH by SW, 60, 211, 268
Vert de Terre 234 by FB, 27, 261
Vesper 70RB67/067 by GL, 206, 249
Vintage Claret 1013 by PL, 124, 213, 253

Walton Cream VM65 by RLP, 160, 248
Warm Sienna 1203 by BM, 87, 220, 252
Waterside 7573M by Parker Paint, 61, 215, 268
Weathered Brown UL44 by RLP, 88, 221, 240
Wedgewood Gray HC-146 by BM, 86, 220, 263
Wendigo 2293 by PL, 99, 224, 242
Wenge AF-180 by BM, 44, 242
Whitall Brown HC-69 by BM, 141, 240
White Chocolate OC-127 by BM, 163, 234
White Dove by BM, 66, 74, 89, 182
White Satin 2067-70 by BM, 121, 267
Whole Wheat SW6121 by SW, 87, 220, 238
Wickham Gray HC-171 by BM, 57
Windham Cream HC-6 by BM, 156, 236
Windmill Wings 2067-60 by BM, 64, 271
Windsor Blue 27-19 by PL, 181, 269
Wintersweet Berry 5104T by FPE, 251
Winter White 2140-70 by BM, 157, 232
Wispy Green 414 by BM, 104, 215, 256
Witke, Bret, Powder Sand 2151-70 by BM, 107
Wolf Gray 2127-40 by BM, 91, 221, 265
Woodlawn Blue HC-147 by BM, 86, 220, 263

Yam 290B-7 by BR, 162, 246
Yellow Gold 758 by GL, 245
Yellow Ground 218 by FB, 99, 224, 245
Yellowhammer GH100 by RLP, 168, 213, 236

PHOTO CREDITS

Christopher Baker: 61, 76, 106

Gordon Beall: 20, 182

John Gould Bessler: 44, 53

Brantley Photography: 66

Courtesy of Chapman
    Radcliff Home: 153

Jonn Coolidge: 79

Roger Davies: 17, 49, 166

Courtesy of Clare Donohue: 86

Pieter Estersohn: 5, 26, 128, 141

Richard Felber: 113

Don Freeman: 2, 14, 30, 36, 46, 54, 63,
    96, 98, 118, 149, 171, 181, 185,
    193, 196

Samuel Frost: 157

J. Savage Gibson: 19, 25, 51

Oberto Gili: 33, 138

Tria Giovan: 70, 110, 115, 132

Sam Gray: 201

Gridley + Graves: 68

Michael Grimm: 73

Ken Hayden: 168

The Estate of David Hicks: 158

Anice Hoachlander/HD Photo: 164

Horst P. Horst/Art + Commerce: 131

Timothy Kolk: 163, 178, 198

Peter Margonelli: 38

Ellen McDermott: 89, 100, 173,
    204-205, 206-207

Jeff McNamara: 56

Karyn Millet: 41, 83, 84, 150, 161

Matthew Millman: 144

Laura Moss: 65

Ngoc Minh Ngo: 78, 90, 123, 126,
    134, 137

Brendan Paul: 29, 147

Eric Piasecki: 80, 103, 154

José Picayo: 58

Michael Price: 74

Lisa Romerein: 42, 92

Lauren Rubinstein: 194

Nathan Schroder: 35

Tim Street-Porter: 81, 105, 176, 188,
    190, 203

Simon Upton: 108

Courtesy of Peter Vaughn: 125

Peter Vitale: 22

Dominique Vorillon: 82

William Waldron: 121, 142

Corey Weiner: 187

Ricky Zehavi: 94